HEROES OF THE SOUTHERN CONFEDERACY

୶୧ THE LOCHLAINN SEABROOK COLLECTION ୨୧

AMERICAN CIVIL WAR
Abraham Lincoln Was a Liberal, Jefferson Davis Was a Conservative: The Missing Key to Understanding the American Civil War
Confederacy 101: Amazing Facts You Never Knew About America's Oldest Political Tradition
Confederate Blood and Treasure: An Interview With Lochlainn Seabrook
Everything You Were Taught About African-Americans and the Civil War is Wrong, Ask a Southerner!
Everything You Were Taught About the Civil War is Wrong, Ask a Southerner!
Give This Book to a Yankee! A Southern Guide to the Civil War For Northerners
Heroes of the Southern Confederacy: The Illustrated Book of Confederate Officials, Soldiers, and Civilians
Lincoln's War: The Real Cause, the Real Winner, the Real Loser
The Great Yankee Coverup: What the North Doesn't Want You to Know About Lincoln's War!
The Ultimate Civil War Quiz Book: How Much Do You Really Know About America's Most Misunderstood Conflict?
Women in Gray: A Tribute to the Ladies Who Supported the Southern Confederacy

CONFEDERATE MONUMENTS
Confederate Monuments: Why Every American Should Honor Confederate Soldiers and Their Memorials

CONFEDERATE FLAG
Confederate Flag Facts: What Every American Should Know About Dixie's Southern Cross
What the Confederate Flag Means to Me: Americans Speak Out in Defense of Southern Honor, Heritage, and History

SECESSION
All We Ask Is To Be Let Alone: The Southern Secession Fact Book

SLAVERY
Everything You Were Taught About American Slavery is Wrong, Ask a Southerner!
Slavery 101: Amazing Facts You Never Knew About America's "Peculiar Institution"

CHILDREN
Honest Jeff and Dishonest Abe: A Southern Children's Guide to the Civil War
Saddle, Sword, and Gun: A Biography of Nathan Bedford Forrest For Teens

NATHAN BEDFORD FORREST
A Rebel Born: A Defense of Nathan Bedford Forrest - Confederate General, American Legend (winner of the 2011 Jefferson Davis Historical Gold Medal)
A Rebel Born: The Screenplay (film about N. B. Forrest)
Forrest! 99 Reasons to Love Nathan Bedford Forrest
Give 'Em Hell Boys! The Complete Military Correspondence of Nathan Bedford Forrest
I Rode With Forrest! Confederate Soldiers Who Served With the World's Greatest Cavalry Leader
Nathan Bedford Forrest and African-Americans: Yankee Myth, Confederate Fact
Nathan Bedford Forrest and the Battle of Fort Pillow: Yankee Myth, Confederate Fact
Nathan Bedford Forrest and the Ku Klux Klan: Yankee Myth, Confederate Fact
Nathan Bedford Forrest: Southern Hero, American Patriot - Honoring a Confederate Icon and the Old South
Saddle, Sword, and Gun: A Biography of Nathan Bedford Forrest For Teens
The God of War: Nathan Bedford Forrest As He Was Seen By His Contemporaries
The Quotable Nathan Bedford Forrest: Selections From the Writings and Speeches of the Confederacy's Most Brilliant Cavalryman

QUOTABLE SERIES
The Alexander H. Stephens Reader: Excerpts From the Works of a Confederate Founding Father
The Quotable Alexander H. Stephens: Selections From the Writings and Speeches of the Confederacy's First Vice President
The Quotable Jefferson Davis: Selections From the Writings and Speeches of the Confederacy's First President
The Quotable Nathan Bedford Forrest: Selections From the Writings and Speeches of the Confederacy's Most Brilliant Cavalryman
The Quotable Robert E. Lee: Selections From the Writings and Speeches of the South's Most Beloved Civil War General
The Quotable Stonewall Jackson: Selections From the Writings and Speeches of the South's Most Famous General
The Unquotable Abraham Lincoln: The President's Quotes They Don't Want You To Know!

CIVIL WAR BATTLES
Encyclopedia of the Battle of Franklin - A Comprehensive Guide to the Conflict that Changed the Civil War
Nathan Bedford Forrest and the Battle of Fort Pillow: Yankee Myth, Confederate Fact
The Battle of Franklin: Recollections of Confederate and Union Soldiers
The Battle of Nashville: Recollections of Confederate and Union Soldiers
The Battle of Spring Hill: Recollections of Confederate and Union Soldiers

CONSTITUTIONAL HISTORY
America's Three Constitutions: Complete Texts of the Articles of Confederation, U.S. Constitution, and C.S. Constitution
The Articles of Confederation Explained: A Clause-by-Clause Study of America's First Constitution
The Constitution of the Confederate States of America Explained: A Clause-by-Clause Study of the South's Magna Carta

VICTORIAN CONFEDERATE LITERATURE
Rise Up and Call Them Blessed: Victorian Tributes to the Confederate Soldier, 1861-1901
Support Your Local Confederate: Wit and Humor in the Southern Confederacy
The God of War: Nathan Bedford Forrest As He Was Seen By His Contemporaries
The Old Rebel: Robert E. Lee As He Was Seen By His Contemporaries
Victorian Confederate Poetry: The Southern Cause in Verse, 1861-1901

ABRAHAM LINCOLN
Abraham Lincoln: The Southern View - Demythologizing America's Sixteenth President
Lincolnology: The Real Abraham Lincoln Revealed in His Own Words - A Study of Lincoln's Suppressed, Misinterpreted, and Forgotten Writings and Speeches
Lincoln's War: The Real Cause, the Real Winner, the Real Loser
The Great Impersonator! 99 Reasons to Dislike Abraham Lincoln
The Unholy Crusade: Lincoln's Legacy of Destruction in the American South
The Unquotable Abraham Lincoln: The President's Quotes They Don't Want You To Know!

NATURAL HISTORY
North America's Amazing Mammals: An Encyclopedia for the Whole Family
The Concise Book of Owls: A Guide to Nature's Most Mysterious Birds
The Concise Book of Tigers: A Guide to Nature's Most Remarkable Cats

PARANORMAL
Carnton Plantation Ghost Stories: True Tales of the Unexplained from Tennessee's Most Haunted Civil War House!
UFOs and Aliens: The Complete Guidebook

FAMILY HISTORIES
The Blakeneys: An Etymological, Ethnological, and Genealogical Study - Uncovering the Mysterious Origins of the Blakeney Family and Name
The Caudills: An Etymological, Ethnological, and Genealogical Study - Exploring the Name and National Origins of a European-American Family
The McGavocks of Carnton Plantation: A Southern History - Celebrating One of Dixie's Most Noble Confederate Families and Their Tennessee Home

MIND, BODY, SPIRIT
Autobiography of a Non-Yogi: A Scientist's Journey From Hinduism to Christianity (Dr. Amitava Dasgupta, with Lochlainn Seabrook)
Britannia Rules: Goddess-Worship in Ancient Anglo-Celtic Society - An Academic Look at the United Kingdom's Matricentric Spiritual Past
Christ Is All and In All: Rediscovering Your Divine Nature and the Kingdom Within
Christmas Before Christianity: How the Birthday of the "Sun" Became the Birthday of the "Son"
Jesus and the Gospel of Q: Christ's Pre-Christian Teachings As Recorded in the New Testament
Jesus and the Law of Attraction: The Bible-Based Guide to Creating Perfect Health, Wealth, and Happiness Following Christ's Simple Formula
Seabrook's Bible Dictionary of Traditional and Mystical Christian Doctrines
The Bible and the Law of Attraction: 99 Teachings of Jesus, the Apostles, and the Prophets
The Book of Kelle: An Introduction to Goddess-Worship and the Great Celtic Mother-Goddess Kelle, Original Blessed Lady of Ireland
The Goddess Dictionary of Words and Phrases: Introducing a New Core Vocabulary for the Women's Spirituality Movement
Vintage Southern Cookbook: Delicious Dishes From Dixie

WOMEN
Aphrodite's Trade: The Hidden History of Prostitution Unveiled
Princess Diana: Modern Day Moon-Goddess - A Psychoanalytical and Mythological Look at Diana Spencer's Life, Marriage, and Death (with Dr. Jane Goldberg)
Women in Gray: A Tribute to the Ladies Who Supported the Southern Confederacy

REPRINTS
A Short History of the Confederate States of America (author Jefferson Davis; editor Lochlainn Seabrook)
Prison Life of Jefferson Davis (author John J. Craven; editor Lochlainn Seabrook)
Life of Beethoven (author Ludwig Nohl; editor Lochlainn Seabrook)
The New Revelation (author Arthur Conan Doyle; editor Lochlainn Seabrook)

Lochlainn Seabrook does not author books for fame and fortune, but for the love of writing and sharing his knowledge.

SeaRavenPress.com

HEROES

OF THE SOUTHERN CONFEDERACY

The Illustrated Book of
Confederate Officials, Soldiers, and Civilians

CONCEIVED, COLLECTED, & ARRANGED, WITH AN INTRODUCTION BY THE AUTHOR,
"THE VOICE OF THE TRADITIONAL SOUTH," COLONEL

LOCHLAINN SEABROOK

JEFFERSON DAVIS HISTORICAL GOLD MEDAL WINNER

Diligently Researched and Generously
Illustrated for the Elucidation of the Reader

2021

Sea Raven Press, Nashville, Tennessee, USA

HEROES OF THE SOUTHERN CONFEDERACY

Published by
Sea Raven Press, Cassidy Ravensdale, President
PO Box 1484, Spring Hill, Tennessee 37174-1484 USA
SeaRavenPress.com • searavenpress@gmail.com

Copyright © text and illustrations Lochlainn Seabrook 2021
in accordance with U.S. and international copyright laws and regulations, as stated and protected under the Berne Union for the Protection of Literary and Artistic Property (Berne Convention), and the Universal Copyright Convention (the UCC). All rights reserved under the Pan-American and International Copyright Conventions.

1st SRP paperback edition, 1st printing, April 2021 • ISBN: 978-1-955351-00-3
1st SRP hardcover edition, 1st printing, April 2021 • ISBN: 978-1-955351-01-0

ISBN: 978-1-955351-00-3 (paperback)
Library of Congress Control Number: 2021936383

This work is the copyrighted intellectual property of Lochlainn Seabrook and has been registered with the Copyright Office at the Library of Congress in Washington, D.C., USA. No part of this work (including text, covers, drawings, photos, illustrations, maps, images, diagrams, etc.), in whole or in part, may be used, reproduced, stored in a retrieval system, or transmitted, in any form or by any means now known or hereafter invented, without written permission from the publisher. The sale, duplication, hire, lending, copying, digitalization, or reproduction of this material, in any manner or form whatsoever, is also prohibited, and is a violation of federal, civil, and digital copyright law, which provides severe civil and criminal penalties for any violations.

> Heroes of the Southern Confederacy: The Illustrated Book of Confederate Officials, Soldiers, and Civilians, by Lochlainn Seabrook. Includes an introduction, index, appendices, footnotes, and bibliography.

Front and back cover design and art, book design, layout, and interior art by Lochlainn Seabrook. All images, image captions, graphic design, & graphic art copyright © Lochlainn Seabrook. All images selected, edited, placed, manipulated, and/or created by Lochlainn Seabrook. Image cleaning, coloration, & tinting by Lochlainn Seabrook. Cover image: Major-General John Brown Gordon, C.S.A., Library of Congress

All persons who approve of the authority and principles of Colonel Lochlainn Seabrook's literary work, and realize its benefits as a means of reeducating the world about the South and the Confederacy, are hereby requested to avidly recommend his books to others and to vigorously cooperate in extending their reach, scope, and influence around the globe.

The views on the American "Civil War" documented in this book are those of the publisher.

PRINTED & MANUFACTURED IN OCCUPIED TENNESSEE, FORMER CONFEDERATE STATES OF AMERICA

DEDICATION

To all those who supported the Confederacy in the 19th Century, and to all those who continue to do so in the 21st Century, this book is reverently dedicated.

EPIGRAPH

The Great Truth

"A people without the memories of heroic suffering or sacrifice are a people without a history."

Major-General John Brown Gordon, C.S.A.
FIRST COMMANDER-IN-CHIEF OF THE UNITED CONFEDERATE VETERANS

CONTENTS

Notes to the Reader - 11
Acknowledgments - 19
Introduction, by Lochlainn Seabrook - 21

SECTION ONE
CONFEDERATE OFFICIALS - 39

SECTION TWO
CONFEDERATE GENERALS - 47

SECTION THREE
CONFEDERATE SOLDIERS & CIVILIANS - 157

Appendix A: Confederate Chain of Command - 293
Appendix B: Information on the Jefferson Davis Cabinet - 295
Appendix C: Supplemental List of Presumed Confederate General Officers - 297
Bibliography - 307
Index - 315
Meet the Author - 323

NOTES TO THE READER

"NOTHING IN THE PAST IS DEAD TO THE MAN WHO WOULD
LEARN HOW THE PRESENT CAME TO BE WHAT IT IS."

William Stubbs, Victorian English Historian

THE TWO MAIN POLITICAL PARTIES IN 1860

☛ In any study of America's antebellum, bellum, and postbellum periods, it is vitally important to understand that in 1860 the two major political parties—the Democrats and the newly formed Republicans—were the opposite of what they are today. In other words, the Democrats of the mid 19th Century were Conservatives, akin to the Republican Party of today, while the Republicans of the mid 19th Century were Liberals, akin to the Democratic Party of today.[1]

The author's cousin, Confederate Vice President and Democrat Alexander H. Stephens: a Southern Conservative.

Thus the Confederacy's Democratic president, Jefferson Davis, was a Conservative (with libertarian leanings); the Union's Republican president, Abraham Lincoln, was a Liberal (with socialistic leanings).[2] This is why, in the mid 1800s, the conservative wing of the Democratic Party was known as "the States' Rights Party."[3]

Hence, the Democrats of the Civil War period referred to themselves as "conservatives," "confederates," "anti-centralists," or "constitutionalists" (the latter because they favored strict adherence to the original Constitution—which tacitly guaranteed states' rights—as created by the Founding Fathers), while the Civil War Republicans called themselves "liberals," "nationalists," "centralists," or "consolidationists" (the latter three because they wanted to nationalize the central

---

1. Woods, p. 47.
2. On Lincoln's socialistic, Marxist, and communist thoughts, ideas, and tendencies, see my books: 1) *Lincoln's War: The Real Cause, The Real Winner, the Real Loser*; 2) *Abraham Lincoln Was a Liberal, Jefferson Davis Was a Conservative: The Missing Key to Understanding the American Civil War*; 3) *Abraham Lincoln: The Southern View*. Also see McCarty, passim; Browder, passim; Benson and Kennedy, passim.
3. See J. W. Jones, TDMV, pp. 144, 200-201, 273.

government and consolidate political power in Washington, D.C.).[4] In 1889 President Davis, who referred to the 1860 Democrats as "the conservative power of the country,"[5] himself explained the political situation at the time this way:

> . . . the names adopted by political parties in the United States have not always been strictly significant of their principles. In general terms it may be said that the old Federal party [Liberal] inclined to nationalism [then a term for big government], or consolidation [that is, consolidation of power in the Federal government], and that the Whig party [liberalistic], which succeeded it, although not identical with it, was favorable, in the main, to a strong Central Government [liberalism and socialism]. On the other hand, its opponent, the Republican [Conservative], afterward known as the Democratic party [until the election of 1896, when the two parties reversed, becoming the parties we know today], was dominated by the idea of the sovereignty of the States and the federal or confederate character of the Union [Americanism or conservatism]. Although other elements have entered into its organization at different periods, this has been its vital, cardinal, and abiding principle.[6]

Since this idea is new to most of my readers, let us further demystify it by viewing it from the perspective of the American Revolutionary War. If Davis and his conservative Southern constituents (the Democrats of 1861) had been alive in 1775, they would have sided with George Washington and the American colonists, who sought to secede from the tyrannical government of Great Britain; if Lincoln and his Liberal Northern constituents (the Republicans of 1861) had been alive at that time, they would have sided with King George III and the English monarchy, who sought to maintain the American colonies as possessions of the British Empire. It is due to this very comparison that we Southerners often refer to our secession from the U.S. as the Second Declaration of Independence and the "Civil War" as the Second American Revolutionary War.

Without a basic understanding of these facts, the American "Civil War" will forever remain incomprehensible. For a full discussion of this topic see my book, *Abraham Lincoln Was a Liberal, Jefferson Davis Was a Conservative: The Missing Key to Understanding the American Civil War.*

---

4. See Seabrook, TAHSR, passim. See also, Pollard, LC, p. 178; J. H. Franklin, pp. 101, 111, 130, 149; Nicolay and Hay, ALCW, Vol. 1, p. 627.
5. Seabrook, ASHCSA (J. Davis), p. 59.
6. Seabrook, ASHCSA (J. Davis), pp. 55-56.

PURPOSE OF THIS BOOK
☛ What this book is meant to be: A straightforward volume preserving some of the photographs, drawings, illustrations, and various other images (whatever their original condition) from the 1800s and early 1900s of my people—the Confederates—before they are lost to history.

What this book is not meant to be: An elaborate, all-inclusive, biographical encyclopedia of every known Confederate officer and soldier, including high quality images, as well as the details of their lives from birth to death—such as their birthplaces, burial locations, spouses' names, children's names, or the armies, corps, divisions, brigades, and regiments they belonged to.

THE IMAGES: SOURCES & QUALITY
☛ Though due to their inclusion in *Heroes of the Southern Confederacy*, these images, photographs, artwork, and illustrations are copyrighted, all originally came from public domain sources—chiefly my personal copies of Evans' massive 12-volume *Confederate Military History*, Miller and Lanier's 10-volume *The Photographic History of the Civil War*, and Johnson and Buel's 4-volume *Battles and Leaders of the Civil War*. I also relied on the voluminous historic collections of the Library of Congress and the National Archives, as well as a myriad of 19th- and early 20th- Century memoirs, histories, biographies, wartime anthologies, and periodicals, such as *Confederate Veteran* and *The Illustrated Confederate War Journal* (also from my personal library).

The illustrations in this book are quite aged—some over 150 years old—and so should not be expected to match the breathtakingly clear high resolution images found in many of today's publications. The antique pictures in my possession range from appallingly blurry to pleasingly sharp, with the majority falling somewhere in between. Speaking as a photographer myself, I enjoy the look of antiquated sepia-toned images. Nonetheless, in this book I have done my best to include the highest quality images possible.

OFFICIAL GENERALSHIP
☛ While I have been careful to follow the basic facts laid out in *General Officers of the Confederate Army* (1911), as well as *Memorandum Relative to the General Officers Appointed by the President in the Armies of the Confederate States, 1861-1865* (1905), the generalship of some of the men listed in my "Confederate Generals" section are, to this day, still in question.

One such individual was Colonel James Hagan. Hagan was referenced in several official documents as an "acting brigadier-general," but the commission for this rank was never confirmed—or perhaps it was confirmed verbally but simply never recorded on paper. In any event, I have given such men the benefit of the doubt and have listed them as generals.

Another example: Thomas Turner Fauntleroy was officially appointed a Confederate brigadier-general in the Provisional Army of Virginia in May 1861. Though the experienced Mexican War veteran subsequently resigned the position in October 1861 (for personal reasons), I have included him in my list in honor of his brief C.S. service.

In other types of dubious cases, where, for instance, men were assigned various ranks that were never officially appointed, I have followed the ranking listings of *Confederate Veteran* magazine. One such gentleman was Mosby Monroe Parsons, a brigadier-general who was later put on duty as a major-general by a superior officer. Unfortunately, President Davis never approved Parson's promotion and to this day he remains listed as a brigadier-general.

Another instance of a Confederate general with a confused rank is William Preston. Though officially appointed a brigadier-general in 1862, he is said to have attained the rank of major-general three years later, in 1865. While no such record of the latter promotion seems to exist, *Confederate Veteran* magazine lists him as a major-general, and thus so do I. A similar fate befell William Booth Taliaferro. Officially a brigadier-general, he left Confederate military service as a major-general. The details concerning *who* promoted him to the latter rank and *when* were never chronicled, which is why some list him as a brigadier-general. *Confederate Veteran* and I register him as a major-general.

Another curious instance concerns Brigadier-General Henry Alexander Wise: though he was eventually given command of a division by General Lee, he was never officially appointed a major-general. Thus he is recorded by *Confederate Veteran*, and by me, as a brigadier-general.

I do not always follow the great and authoritative *Confederate Veteran*, however. One such case concerns my close kinsman Edmund Winchester Rucker. Starting off as a Confederate colonel, Rucker was later appointed brigadier-general. Unfortunately, his commission did not arrive until after the War and it is therefore deemed by some as "unofficial" (among them *Confederate Veteran*). In honor of his gallant service under Lieutenant-General Nathan Bedford Forrest (during which Rucker lost an arm as a result of the Battle of Nashville)—as well as a deserving tribute to one of my family names (I descend from the Ruckers of Virginia, making Edmund and I third cousins)—I have included him in this work as a brigadier-general.

CONFEDERATES IN U.S. MILITARY GEAR
☞ For the most part the C.S.A. army and navy operated on a shortage of supplies, and for a myriad of reasons, from damaged railroads and factories, to financial and commissary issues, as well as Lincoln's illegal blockade. Thus, out of necessity many Confederate soldiers were forced to outfit themselves with hand-me-downs from what General Forrest wittily called "Uncle Sam's Larder," that is, Yankee troops.[7] Both Yankee captives and Yankee corpses were considered fair game.

The result was that it was not uncommon for a Confederate soldier to appear on the battlefield completely or partially uniformed in Union blue, which often included a U.S. rifle, kepi, belt, and canteen. This will explain why some of the Confederate soldiers in *Heroes of the Southern Confederacy* are sporting various Yankee accoutrements.

A WORD ON EARLY AMERICAN MATERIAL
☞ In order to preserve the authentic historicity of the antebellum, bellum, and postbellum periods, I have retained the original spellings, formatting, and punctuation of 19th-Century literature. These include such items as "major-general" rather than the modern spelling, "major general," as well as British-English spellings, long-running paragraphs, obsolete words, and various literary devices peculiar to the time. However, I have corrected misspelled names to prevent confusion, and also *where possible*, inaccurate dates and locations (the inevitable result of old faulty memories). Bracketed words within quotes are my additions and clarifications, while italicized words within quotes are (where indicated) my emphasis.

PRESENTISM
☞ As a historian I view *presentism* (judging the past according to present day mores and customs) as the enemy of authentic history. And this is precisely why the Left employs it in its ongoing war against traditional American, conservative, and Christian values. By looking at history through the lens of modern day beliefs—and, just as heinous,

Judging our ancestors by our own standards is dishonest, unfair, unjust, misleading, and unethical.

---

7. Lochlainn Seabrook, *A Rebel Born: A Defense of Nathan Bedford Forrest*, Franklin, TN: Sea Raven Press, 2015 ed., pp. 340, 489, 515.

fabricating obviously fake history based on emotion, opinion, and political ideology—they are able to distort, revise, and reshape the past into a false narrative that fits their ideological agenda: the liberalization *and* Northernization of America, the enlargement and further centralization of the national government, and total control of American political, economic, and social power, the same agenda that Lincoln championed.[8]

This book, like all of my other titles, rejects presentism and replaces it with what I call *historicalism*: judging our ancestors based on the values of their own time. To get the most from this work the reader is invited to reject presentism as well. In this way—along with casting aside preconceived notions and the fake history churned out by our left-wing education system—the truth in this work will be most readily ascertained and absorbed; truth that has been rigorously researched and forensically uncovered by myself using the scientific method. As Confederate Colonel Bennett H. Young noted in 1901:

> History is valuable only as it is true. Opinions concerning acts are not history; acts themselves alone are historic.[9]

LEARN MORE

☞ Lincoln's War on the Constitution and the American people can never be fully understood without a thorough knowledge of the South's perspective. As this book is only meant to be a brief introductory guide to these topics, one cannot hope to learn the complete story here. For those who are interested in additional material from Dixie's viewpoint, please see my comprehensive histories listed on pages 2 and 3. L.S.

---

8. For more on the nihilistic, atheistic, anti-life, anti-tradition, anti-American, anti-Constitution, anti-capitalism, anti-South agenda of the Victorian Republican Party (then the Liberal Party) and the modern Democrat Party (now the Liberal Party), otherwise known as "The Communist/Socialist Rules for Revolution," see Hasselring, pp. 2350-2351; Lenin, passim; Marx and Engels, passim; B. Dodd, passim. Also see my book *What the Confederate Flag Means to Me: Americans Speak Out in Defense of Southern Honor, Heritage, and History*. Spring Hill, TN: Sea Raven Press, 2021.
9. *Confederate Veteran*, July 1901, Vol. 9, No. 7, p. 318.

Keep Your Body, Mind, & Spirit Vibrating at Their Highest Level

YOU CAN DO SO BY READING THE BOOKS OF

SEA RAVEN PRESS

There is nothing that will so perfectly keep your body, mind, and spirit in a healthy condition as to think wisely and positively. Hence you should not only read this book, but also the other books that we offer. They will quicken your physical, mental, and spiritual vibrations, enabling you to maintain a position in society as a healthy erudite person.

KEEP YOURSELF WELL-INFORMED!

The well-informed person is always at the head of the procession, while the ignorant, the lazy, and the unthoughtful hang onto the rear. If you are a Spiritual man or woman, do yourself a great favor: read Sea Raven Press books and stay well posted on the Truth. It is almost criminal for one to remain in ignorance while the opportunity to gain knowledge is open to all at a nominal price.

We invite you to visit our Webstore for a wide selection of wholesome, family-friendly, well-researched, educational books for all ages. You will be glad you did!

Five-Star Books & Gifts From the Heart of the American South

SeaRavenPress.com

"I believe it is the duty of every Confederate whose opportunities are such as to enable him to speak now, with anything like accuracy, to put on record what he knows. He owes this duty not only to himself and his associates, but to the truth."

BRIGADIER-GENERAL JOHNSON HAGOOD, C.S.A.
1871

ACKNOWLEDGMENTS

A SPECIAL THANK YOU TO THE AUTHORS OF AND CONTRIBUTORS TO

- *Confederate Veteran*
- *Confederate Military History*
- *The Illustrated Confederate War Journal*
- *Blue and Gray*
- *Southern Historical Society Papers*
- *Battles and Leaders of the Civil War*
- *The Photographic History of the Civil War*
- *Journal of the Congress of the Confederate States of America*

AND THE STAFF AT

- *The National Archives*
- *The Library of Congress*

**as well as the authors and editors
of the many titles in my bibliography**

*for providing both the biographical data and
the majority of the illustrations in this volume.*

I also owe a debt of gratitude to the

HUNDREDS OF UNNAMED
19TH-CENTURY AND EARLY 20TH-CENTURY
PHOTOGRAPHERS AND ARTISTS

(in particular daguerreian Charles R. Rees)

whose poignant and beautiful images fill this book.

"Books invite all; they constrain none."
Hartley Burr Alexander (1873-1939)

INTRODUCTION

"AFTER THE CONVENTION OF 1787, THESE DIFFERENCES CULMINATED, IN 1861, IN BLOOD, BUT NOT IN TREASON."

John Witherspoon DuBose 1892

IT IS MY GREAT HONOR to present this illustrated volume to the public; one that celebrates some of the most intrepid, enterprising, learned individuals the world has ever known: the men and women of the Confederate States of America.

WHY I WROTE THIS BOOK
Though a "book of pictures," this is no idle work. In fact, its true significance will only be appreciated after a thorough and studious perusal of its pages—which contain, among other things, copious detailed and priceless material that will be of interest to researchers.

Its value will be further enhanced by the realization that the authentic history of the C.S.A. has been virtually rewritten from beginning to end by the victor of Lincoln's War (the political Left). Indeed, every vestige that proves its existence—and more importantly, every piece of evidence that chronicles the Truth about the Southern Cause—is being methodically and nefariously removed from our history books, libraries, bookstores, schools, colleges, universities, and online records.

Thus, *Heroes of the Southern Confederacy* is largely a work of preservation, and this was my primary impetus for conceiving, writing, and compiling it.

SOUTHERN CULTURE IS UNDER CONSTANT ATTACK
Like nearly everything else connected to the C.S.A., visual images of the courageous Southern Conservatives (and some right-wing Yankees) who stood up to the tyrannical progressive North in the mid 19th Century have also been demonized, and so are disappearing at an alarming rate.

The Left's goal here of course is to eventually completely wipe out the memory of the C.S.A., and to do this every trace must first be demonized, then secondly obliterated. Hence the ongoing destruction, defilement, and elimination of Confederate monuments, Confederate statues, Confederate cemeteries, Confederate paintings, Confederate flags, Confederate symbols, and Confederate memorabilia from every government owned facility, from U.S. public schools and military bases to museums and the halls of Congress.

THE TRUTHS MY BOOK PRESERVES
By saving the images of Confederate men, women, and children in book form I am creating a small bulwark against the massive cultural genocide now taking place against my people—the Southern people, whatever their race—and our shared 500 year history. This book will provide demonstrable factual verification to future generations that the Confederacy once existed; that it had been legally established; that as Conservatives the Southern people were the *true* patriots in the War of 1861; that they were a righteous, law-abiding, compassionate people who only took up arms defensively (rather than offensively) in order to halt the illegal invasion of their homeland; and finally to prove that their cause was Americanism—the very bedrock of the U.S. Constitution as conceived by the Founding Fathers.[10]

Now to the images themselves and the amazing and fascinating Victorian individuals they portray.

SECTION ONE: CONFEDERATE OFFICIALS
The first segment of *Heroes of the Southern Confederacy* is devoted to President Jefferson Davis' cabinet, with each member's image being accompanied by his personal name, position, birth year, and death year.

Many people are not aware that despite the fact that there were only six positions, 18 individuals served in this governmental body. The high turnover rate was due to the constantly shifting conditions that resulted from both Lincoln's election and his sudden invasion of Dixie, which necessitated setting up a hitherto nonexistent government in only a few months—complete with all of the necessary branches, departments, and personnel, as well as a fully equipped army and navy.

SECTION TWO: CONFEDERATE GENERALS
The second portion of my volume comprises a complete list, or as close as one can get to a complete list when it comes to Lincoln's War, of every known Confederate who *legally* attained the rank of general. According to the C.S. chain of command, this includes brigadier-generals, major-generals, lieutenant-generals, and full generals. As with President Davis' cabinet members, I have provided each general's personal name, rank, birth year, and death year.

In creating my list of generals, I have followed the authoritative compilations of Confederate veterans whenever possible, only adding a few individuals who I believe were left out either by mistake or unfairly. (I have noted my additions in Appendix C.)

As I suggest in my "Notes to the Reader," there is still no full consensus among historians on exactly who belongs or does not belong on this list, and questions also remain regarding the official rank of many of the men. Thus we must content ourselves with the 156 year old

---

10. For more on these topics, see my works listed on pages 2 and 3.

information we have at hand, and my list, I believe, represents one of the most accurate compendiums of Confederate generals available.

CAUSES OF DEATH AMONG CONFEDERATES

Obviously, most of the Confederate officers and soldiers with death dates that fall between 1861 and 1865 perished in the War, sometimes suffering instant death, as in the case of Brigadier-General George Pierce Doles (who was shot down by a Yankee sharpshooter near Bethesda Church in 1864), or dying later from their surgeries, infections, or separate but related illnesses, such as Lieutenant-General Stonewall Jackson (who succumbed to pneumonia in 1863 after having his wounded arm amputated). Sometimes, however, an individual died during the conflict from unrelated causes. Brigadier-General Philip St. George Cocke, for example, took his own life in December 1861; Brigadier-General Claudius Charles Wilson died from "camp fever" in 1863; Brigadier-General Lucius Marshall Walker was killed in a pistol dual in 1863; and Brigadier-General John Henry Winder perished in early 1865, a few months before war's end, from stress and exhaustion.

CONFEDERATE FARMERS

It is interesting to note the professions of those Confederate generals who survived the War for Southern Independence. Many simply returned to the quiet lives they had been living prior to the conflict. Often they craved and needed (both psychologically and physically) the peaceful life of the gentleman farmer, and as such pursued a life of agriculture, men like:

- Major-General Thomas Lafayette Rosser.
- Brigadier-General William McComb.
- Major-General Edward Johnson.
- Brigadier-General John Stuart Williams.
- Major-General Lunsford Lindsay Lomax.
- Brigadier-General Bryan Morel Thomas.
- Brigadier-General Alfred Jefferson Vaughan Jr., who farmed for many years after the War and who (like the author) was a strong supporter of the Grange movement.
- Lieutenant-General Nathan Bedford Forrest.
- Lieutenant-General William Joseph Hardee.
- Brigadier-General Alfred Eugene Jackson.
- Brigadier-General Stand Watie.
- Brigadier-General Hylan Benton Lyon.
- Brigadier-General Reuben Lindsay Walker.
- Brigadier-General Thomas Moore Scott.
- Brigadier-General James Argyle Smith.
- Brigadier-General James Patrick Major.
- Lieutenant-General Theophilus Hunter Holmes.

Confederate Brigadier-General William Hicks Jackson, who married one of my close cousins (Selene Harding)[11] and who eventually served as president of both the Tennessee Bureau of Agriculture and the National Agricultural Congress, bred and developed thoroughbred horses at Belle Meade Plantation here in Nashville (built by my cousin John Harding in 1807). General Robert E. Lee's second son, Confederate Major-General William Henry Fitzhugh Lee, devoted much of his time to farming after the War and served a stint as president of the Virginia Agricultural Society.

CONFEDERATE RAILROAD MEN
As members of my own family did in Kentucky in the mid 20th Century, after the War many former Confederates worked (either part-time or permanently) in the Southern railroad business. Such men included:

• Brigadier-General Reuben Lindsay Walker.
• Brigadier-General Sterling Alexander Martin Wood.
• Lieutenant-General Nathan Bedford Forrest.
• Brigadier-General William Tatum Wofford.
• Brigadier-General Williams Carter Wickham.

CONFEDERATE EDUCATORS
General Robert E. Lee would have preferred a bucolic life himself. Nonetheless, he was coaxed into serving as president of Washington College (now Washington and Lee University). His first son, former Confederate Major-General George Washington Custis Lee, took over his father's position at the time of the great chieftain's death in 1870. Their ambitious cousin, Lieutenant-General Stephen Dill Lee, became a postwar farmer, state senator, the first president of Mississippi State College, and Commander-in-Chief of the United Confederate Veterans.

Education had a special attraction to many other postwar Confederate generals as well. No doubt most intuitively understood that the Leftist victor would rewrite the history of the War in order to justify its actions, many of them criminal and therefore illegal (the generals' predictions turned out to be accurate). Among these ex-Confederates were:

• Brigadier-General George Doherty Johnston, who served as commandant of cadets at the University of Alabama, as well as superintendent of the South Carolina Military Academy.
• Lieutenant-General Alexander Peter Stewart, a former professor at Cumberland University, who served as chancellor of the University of Mississippi.
• Brigadier-General Mark Perrin Lowrey, who founded, and served as president of, the Blue Mountain Female Institute.
• Brigadier-General Lawrence Sullivan Ross, who served as the president

---

11. I descend from the Harding family.

of the Agricultural and Mechanical College of Texas from 1891 to 1898.
- Brigadier-General Josiah Gorgas (the creator of the Confederate Ordnance Department), who became vice-chancellor of the University of the South in 1868 and president of the University of Alabama in 1878.
- Major-General Bushrod Rust Johnson, who served as chancellor of the University of Nashville in 1870.
- Lieutenant-General Daniel Harvey Hill, who served as president of the University of Arkansas (1877-1884) as well as president of the Middle Georgia Military and Agricultural College (1886-1889).

SOME CONFEDERATE OFFICERS OF NOTE
A number of luminaries are to be found in the list of our Confederate generals. Among them:

- Brigadier-General James Edwin Slaughter, a great-nephew of Founding Father and U.S. President James Madison.
- Brigadier-General Henry Hopkins Sibley, the inventor of the famous Sibley tent.
- Lieutenant-General Richard Taylor, son of U.S. President Zachary Taylor and the brother of Jefferson Davis' first wife, Sarah Knox Taylor.
- Brigadier-General Gabriel James Rains, who invented the first antipersonnel mine.
- Lieutenant-General John Clifford Pemberton, the uncle of Confederate Lieutenant-Colonel John Stith Pemberton, who invented Coca-Cola on May 8, 1886, at Atlanta, Georgia.
- Lieutenant-General Nathan Bedford Forrest, a self-made multimillionaire who is still considered the world's greatest cavalry leader.[12]

CONFEDERATE LITERARY MEN
Many former Confederate officers took up writing, or were writers before the War and returned to the occupation afterward. This list includes such individuals as:

- Brigadier-General Henry Constantine Wayne.
- Major-General Samuel Gibbs French.
- Brigadier-General John Creed Moore.
- Major-General Dabney Herndon Maury (founder of the Southern Historical Society).
- Brigadier-General Henry Alexander Wise.
- Brigadier-General Armistead Lindsay Long.
- Major-General John Brown Gordon (Gordon, whose photo graces the

---

12. For more on the life and times of nearly everyone's favorite Confederate officer, see my 12 books on Forrest.

front cover of this book, helped organize the United Confederate Veterans, which begat *Confederate Veteran* magazine, and later the Sons of Confederate Veterans—to which I belong).
- Major-General Gustavus Woodson Smith.
- Brigadier-General Edward Porter Alexander.
- Brigadier-General Basil Wilson Duke.
- Brigadier-General Marcus Joseph Wright.
- General John Bell Hood.
- Brigadier-General Adam Rankin Johnson.
- Lieutenant-General James Longstreet.
- Brigadier-General Gilbert Moxley Sorrel.

CONFEDERATE POLITICIANS
As referenced above, a number of former Confederates went into, or returned to, politics in the postbellum period. Democrat (a Conservative at the time) Major-General Joseph Wheeler, for instance, was elected for eight consecutive terms as an Alabama Representative, serving from the 47th Congress to the 55th Congress (1881-1899), nearly 20 years. Not only this, Wheeler was also elected to the U.S. House of Representatives and fought in the Spanish-American War (1898)—having been appointed a U.S. military officer by President William McKinley. (The former Confederate's command oversaw a U.S. cavalry division that included the famed regiment known as Theodore "Roosevelt's Rough Riders.")

General Wheeler's late Victorian Era political career bears overt witness to the fact that the fabricated negative stigma that the modern Left has attached to 19th- and early 20th-Century Confederates was almost nonexistent in the postwar world. Let us look at a few more examples:

- In 1886 former Confederate Major-General Cadmus Marcellus Wilcox was given an appointment in a division of the U.S. Land Office by President Grover Cleveland.
- Former Confederate Brigadier-General Alexander Robert Lawton was appointed minister to Austria by President Cleveland in 1887.
- Former Confederate Brigadier-General Francis Marion Cockrell was appointed to the U.S. Interstate Commerce Commission by President Theodore Roosevelt.
- Former Confederate Major-General Dabney Herndon Maury served four years as U.S. minister to Columbia.
- Former Confederate Brigadier-General John Crawford Vaughn served as a presiding officer in the Tennessee senate.
- Former Confederate Brigadier-General Charles Miller Shelley served as a sheriff and a congressman and was later appointed an auditor of the U.S. Department of the Treasury by President Cleveland.
- Former Confederate Brigadier-General Matt Whitaker Ransom served as a U.S. senator and was appointed minister to Mexico by President Cleveland.
- Former Confederate Brigadier-General Joseph Orville Shelby was

appointed U.S. marshal for the Western District by President Cleveland in 1893.
- Former Confederate Brigadier-General John Tyler Morgan served as an Alabama state senator.
- Former Confederate Brigadier-General Henry Rootes Jackson was appointed minister to Mexico by President Cleveland in 1885.
- Former Brigadier-General Lawrence Sullivan Ross, who served as a Texas state senator in 1881 and 1883 and later, in 1887, as governor of Texas.
- Former Confederate Major-General Fitzhugh Lee, who was elected governor of Virginia in 1885, appointed consul-general at Havana, Cuba, by President Cleveland, and was later asked to retain the position by President McKinley.
- Former Confederate Brigadier-General George Earl Maney served numerous diplomatic posts for the U.S. government throughout South America.
- Former Confederate Brigadier-General Gabriel Colvin Wharton served several terms in Virginia's state legislature.
- Former Confederate Brigadier-General Robert Brank Vance served in Washington, D.C. as an assistant commissioner of patents, a congressman (six terms), and a North Carolina state representative.
- Former Confederate Major-General William Henry Fitzhugh Lee served as a Virginia state senator for four years.
- Former Confederate Brigadier-General William Henry Wallace served for nearly two decades in South Carolina's House of Representatives.
- Former Confederate Major-General Samuel Bell Maxey served as a Texas state senator for two terms.
- Former Confederate Brigadier-General Robert Lowry served as both a state senator and the governor of Mississippi.
- Former Confederate Brigadier-General James Alexander Walker served as a Virginia house delegate, lieutenant-governor of Virginia, and a member of the U.S. House of Representatives.
- Former Confederate Brigadier-General Edward Lloyd Thomas worked in the U.S. Land Department and the U.S. Indian Bureau, both positions appointed by President Cleveland.
- Former Confederate Brigadier-General Lucius Eugene Polk served as a Tennessee senator.
- Former Confederate Brigadier-General Alfred Moore Scales served in the U.S. government continuously for 23 years (from 1866 to 1889), first as a member of the North Carolina Legislature, second as a member of the U.S. House of Representatives, and third as governor of North Carolina.
- Former Confederate Major-General Edward Cary Walthall served as a U.S. senator from Mississippi for 13 years.
- Former Confederate Major-General John George Walker served as U.S. consul-general at Bogota, Columbia.
- Former Confederate Brigadier-General Daniel Chevillette Govan was

appointed Indian Agent of the State of Washington by President Cleveland in 1894.

POSTWAR YANKS HIRED FORMER CONFEDERATES
A number of Southern officers were hired by their former Northern enemies after the War. One example was Confederate Major-General James Fleming Fagan, who, in 1875, was appointed United States Marshal by former Union General and U.S. President Ulysses S. Grant.

FORMER CONFEDERATES & THE U.S. GOVERNMENT
Many Confederate officers worked for the U.S. government either as politicians or as military men (sometimes both) before *and* after the War. This list includes:

- Confederate Major-General William Smith, who served as antebellum governor of Virginia from 1846 to 1849, and as postbellum governor of Virginia in 1865.
- Confederate Major-General Jones Mitchell Withers, who served as mayor of Mobile, Alabama, before and after the conflict.
- Confederate Brigadier-General Sterling Alexander Martin Wood, who served as a member of the Alabama legislature antebellum and postbellum.
- Confederate Brigadier-General John Wilkins Whitfield, who, before Lincoln's War, fought in the Mexican-American War as a U.S. officer and served as a Kansas congressman; after Lee's surrender General Whitfield served as a Texas state representative.
- Confederate Brigadier-General John Stuart Williams, who served in the Kentucky legislature before and after the War.

Some, like fiery secessionist Confederate Brigadier-General Louis Trezevant Wigfall, served in the U.S. government (as a legislator and a senator) prior to the War but not afterward. Similarly, Confederate Brigadier-General Robert Augustus Toombs served in both congressional houses before the War, but did not reenter U.S. politics postbellum: a passionate states' rights advocate, he permanently disqualified himself from office by refusing to apply for a "pardon" from the United States. Brigadier-General Henry Alexander Wise was also heavily involved in U.S. politics before Lincoln's War, serving as a congressman, minister to Brazil, and governor of Virginia. Afterward, however, the strongly conservative constitutionalist disavowed any allegiance to the U.S. government.

MORE CONFEDERATES IN THE U.S. GOVERNMENT
Other former C.S. generals, too numerous to mention, also served in important positions within the U.S. government *after* Lincoln's War. Here are a few examples:

- Former Confederate Brigadier-General Basil Wilson Duke, who worked

as a commissioner of Shiloh National Military Park for 21 years.
- Former Confederate Brigadier-General Allen Thomas, who served as U.S. consul and minister to Venezuela.
- Former Confederate Brigadier-General Thomas Hart Taylor, who served as a deputy U.S. marshal and as a police chief.
- Former Confederate Brigadier-General Edmund Winston Pettus, who served as an Alabama senator for several terms.
- Former Confederate Lieutenant-General Alexander Peter Stewart, who served as a commissioner of the Chickamauga and Chattanooga National Military Park.
- Former Confederate Brigadier-General Edward Asbury O'Neal, who served two terms as governor of Alabama.
- Former Confederate Major-General Lunsford Lindsay Lomax, who served as a commissioner of the Gettysburg National Military Park.
- Former Confederate Major-General James Lawson Kemper, who served as governor of Virginia from 1874-1877.
- Former Confederate Brigadier-General William Terry, who served two terms as a U.S. congressman and later acted as a Democratic (then the Conservative party) delegate to the National Convention in 1880.
- Former Confederate Brigadier-General Benjamin Grubb Humphreys, who served as governor of Mississippi.
- Former Confederate Brigadier-General John Doby Kennedy, who was appointed consul general at Shanghai by President Cleveland in 1885.
- Former Confederate Brigadier-General Bryan Morel Thomas, a superintendent of public schools and a deputy U.S. marshal.
- Former Confederate Brigadier-General Randall Lee Gibson, who became a U.S. senator.
- Former Confederate Lieutenant-General James Longstreet, who served as the commissioner of Pacific railroads during both William McKinley's and Theodore Roosevelt's administrations.
- Former Confederate Brigadier-General Alfred Holt Colquitt, who was elected governor of Georgia in 1876.
- Former Confederate Brigadier-General Thomas Fentress Toon, who served as North Carolina's state superintendent of public instruction.
- Former Confederate Brigadier-General Francis Redding Tillou Nicholls, who served several terms as governor of Louisiana.
- Former Confederate Brigadier-General Nathaniel Harrison Harris, who served as Administrator of the U.S. Land Office at Aberdeen, South Dakota.
- Former Confederate Brigadier-General Johnson Hagood, who was elected governor of South Carolina in 1880.
- Former Confederate Brigadier-General William Polk Hardeman, who served as assistant sergeant-at-arms of the Texas House of Representatives.
- Former Confederate Major-General Lafayette McLaws, who served for several years as U.S. postmaster at Savannah, Georgia.
- Former Confederate Brigadier-General James Edwin Slaughter, who

served as U.S. postmaster at Mobile, Alabama.
- Former Confederate Major-General Joseph Brevard Kershaw, who served as a U.S. senator, a judge, and a postmaster.
- Former Confederate Lieutenant-General Wade Hampton, who was elected governor of South Carolina in 1876 and was reelected in 1878, became a U.S. Senator in 1879, and served for five years (1893-1899) as Commissioner of Pacific Railways.

Those who worked in lesser roles in the U.S. political machine include:

- Former Confederate Brigadier-General Thomas Harrison, who served as a Democratic (then conservative) Presidential Elector in 1872.
- Former Confederate Major-General Harry Thompson Hays, who served as the sheriff of Orleans Parish in Louisiana in 1866.
- Former Confederate Brigadier-General Thomas Muldrup Logan, who served as the chairman of Virginia's "Gold Democrat" party in 1896.
- Former Confederate Lieutenant-General Nathan Bedford Forrest, who served as a Tennessee alderman, a sheriff, and a delegate at the Democratic National Convention in 1868.[13]
- Former Confederate Brigadier-General Eppa Hunton, who served as a member of the Electoral Commission, the Senate, and the national House of Representatives.

Though not a general, when it came to returning to the Old Union and working for the U.S. government, former Confederate Vice-President Alexander Hamilton Stephens (who had previously worked in the U.S. government from 1836 to 1859) may have outdone them all: Conservative Stephens served the Union at Washington, D.C., in one official political capacity or another, from 1866 until his death in 1883. Thus the great Confederate official devoted a total of 40 years of his life to U.S. politics.

CONFEDERATES WHO WERE MEXICAN WAR VETERANS

The most blatant example of Confederate officers who worked for the U.S. government during the antebellum period were those who fought as U.S. soldiers during the Mexican-American War (1846-1848). Many could be named, but the most famous of these are Confederate General Robert E. Lee and Confederate Lieutenant-General Stonewall Jackson. A few other illustrious individuals in this category are:

- Confederate General Braxton Bragg.
- Confederate Brigadier-General Adley Hogan Gladden.
- Confederate Brigadier-General John Henry Winder.
- Confederate Brigadier-General Henry Hopkins Sibley.

---

13. For a detailed account of the life story of "ole Bedford," see my award-winning Forrest biography: *A Rebel Born: A Defense of Nathan Bedford Forrest*, Franklin, TN: Sea Raven Press, 2015 ed.

- Confederate Brigadier-General John Crawford Vaughn.
- Confederate Brigadier-General Montgomery Dent Corse.
- Confederate Major-General Harry Thompson Hays.
- Confederate Major-General John George Walker.
- Confederate Brigadier-General William Whann Mackall.
- Confederate Brigadier-General Henry Alexander Wise.
- Confederate Brigadier-General Robert Hall Chilton.
- Confederate Major-General Earl Van Dorn.
- Confederate Brigadier-General Lewis Henry Little.
- Confederate Brigadier-General Gideon Johnson Pillow.
- Confederate Brigadier-General Edward Lloyd Thomas.
- Confederate Brigadier-General Henry Constantine Wayne.

While their four-year service as Confederates (that is, Conservatives) alone should make them immortal American patriots in the eyes of the world, their additional work in the U.S. government—both antebellum and postbellum—means that these men should be doubly honored in our history books for their dedication to both republics: the Confederate States of America and the United States of America.

Yet, despite their honorable service, as well as their lifelong devotion to our country and its foundational document, the U.S. Constitution, the statues, busts, names, and portraits of these brave men are being removed from all governmental buildings—due merely to un-historical falsehoods intentionally invented and spread by the radical Left.

FORMER CONFEDERATE SOLDIERS WHO WENT LEFT
Though the Southern Confederacy was a Conservative government founded by Democrats (then the Conservative party), and while most Confederate soldiers were also politically conservative, after the War several Confederate veterans joined the Left-wing and became Republicans (then the Liberal party). Among these were Brigadier-General Rufus Barringer, Lieutenant-General James Longstreet (a personal friend of Grant), Brigadier-General Williams Carter Wickham, and Brigadier-General George Earl Maney.

FORMER CONFEDERATES WHO REJOINED THE U.S. MILITARY
As I have shown, and as all serious students of history are aware, many Confederate officers served in the U.S. military prior to Lincoln's War. However, it is often overlooked that a number of former Confederate officers joined the U.S. military *again* after the War. Such individuals included Confederate Major-General Matthew Calbraith Butler, as well as former Confederate Major-General Thomas Lafayette Rosser of Virginia, a youngster who had been attending the United States Military Academy (West Point) in New York when Lincoln's War broke out. In 1898, 33 years after the hostilities had subsided, President McKinley appointed him a brigadier-general of the U.S. Volunteers.

YANKEES IN THE CONFEDERATE RANKS

Many Confederate officers were Yankees by birth—though Southern by heart and mind. Most of these men, from Northern or Western states, recognized the importance of states' rights and preserving the Constitution of the Founding Generation. Among these were:

- Confederate Brigadier-General Albert Pike of Massachusetts.
- Confederate Brigadier-General William Stephen Walker of Pennsylvania.
- Confederate Brigadier-General Allen Thomas of Maryland.
- Confederate Brigadier-General Walter Husted Stevens of New York.
- Confederate Lieutenant-General John Clifford Pemberton of Pennsylvania.
- Confederate Brigadier-General Lawrence Sullivan Ross of Iowa.
- Confederate Brigadier-General Francis Asbury Shoup of Indiana.
- Confederate Major-General Martin Luther Smith of New York.
- Confederate Brigadier-General Edward Aylesworth Perry of Massachusetts.
- Confederate Brigadier-General Charles Sidney Winder of Maryland.
- Confederate Brigadier-General William McComb of Pennsylvania.
- Confederate Brigadier-General William Steele of New York.
- Confederate Brigadier-General George Hume Steuart of Maryland.
- Confederate Brigadier-General Albert Gallatin Blanchard of Massachusetts.
- Confederate Brigadier-General Clement Hoffman Stevens of Connecticut.
- Confederate Brigadier-General Zebulon York of Maine.
- Confederate Major-General Lunsford Lindsay Lomax of Rhode Island.
- Confederate Major-General Mansfield Lovell of Washington, D.C.
- Confederate Brigadier-General Lewis Henry Little of Maryland.
- Confederate Brigadier-General Claudius Wistar Sears of Massachusetts.
- Confederate Major-General Samuel Gibbs French of New Jersey.
- Confederate Brigadier-General Robert Hopkins Hatton of Ohio.
- Confederate General Samuel Cooper of New York.
- Confederate Brigadier-General Daniel Ruggles of Massachusetts.
- Confederate Brigadier-General Danville Leadbetter of Maine.

SECTION THREE: CONFEDERATE SOLDIERS & CIVILIANS

The third and final section of this volume focuses on both the Confederate soldier (of all ranks below general) and the Confederate civilian: man, woman, and child.

Many of these photographs are of Confederates who have not been identified. Nearly half are recognized and named, however. In all cases I have supplied each image with personal names, the approximate date they were created, and rank—where appropriate and known.

Naturally, the images in this section are of a much more personal and emotional nature than those found in Section One (the Confederate cabinet) and Section Two (Confederate generals). Indeed, lower ranked military men often posed not only with fellow soldiers, but also with their family members, friends, sweethearts, and wives. One enlisted man posed with his dog.

More generally, however, soldiers sat singly for the photographer in creative sessions that called for a menacing countenance, complete with all manner of bristling weaponry—the better to instill dread and misgiving in the Yankee heart.

Despite the well-known Southern courage and fearlessness evinced in most of these portraits, several Confederate soldiers are holding, not Bowie knives, Colt pistols, or Sharps rifles, but flowers; perhaps in honor of a loved one; or as a hopeful sign that logic, law, and common sense would prevail and that peace with the North (as artificial as it had been for decades) would soon return.

Such was not to be, of course.

Lincoln turned down *every* effort on behalf of Davis and the C.S.A. to establish a compromise on which the war could be brought to a speedy end. Why? Because, like those on the radical Left today, "Honest Abe" and his socialist administrators (such as Charles A. Dana) and communist Union generals (like August Willich)—many of them personal friends of Karl Marx, the founder of modern communism—needed the social, political, and economic disruption and racial division that the war engendered in order to instigate their villainous agenda: the elimination of states' rights, the Northernization (and thus the destruction) of the South, and the eventual establishment of an all powerful central government at Washington, headed by a Liberal cabinet with socialist goals.[14]

While Lincoln did not live to see his plan to fruition, he would be more than delighted to know that 156 years later at least one aspect of his cultural Marxist goals has largely been achieved: the complete demonization of the South, along with the slow but gradual elimination of her culture, heritage, symbols, heroes, and history.[15]

WHAT THIS BOOK REVEALS

By writing this book I aim to help counter this evil and corrosive plot. In the process, my illustrations will reveal, as nothing else can, that the Confederate was not a "racist," a "traitor," or a "violent uneducated hayseed," as the ill-informed continue to assert.

To begin with, the hundreds of thousands of Southern men who enlisted in the Confederate military would have never lifted a finger to "save slavery." Indeed, the American abolition movement got its start in

---

14. For more on these topics see my books: 1) *Abraham Lincoln Was a Liberal, Jefferson Davis Was a Conservative: The Missing Key to Understanding the American Civil War.* Spring Hill, TN: Sea Raven Press, 2017; 2) *Lincoln's War: The Real Cause, the Real Winner, the Real Loser.* Spring Hill, TN: Sea Raven Press, 2016.

15. For more on Lincoln and his War see my books: 1) *Abraham Lincoln: The Southern View.* 2007. Franklin, TN: Sea Raven Press, 2013 ed.; 2) *The Unholy Crusade: Lincoln's Legacy of Destruction in the American South.* Spring Hill, TN: Sea Raven Press, 2017; 3) *Lincolnology: The Real Abraham Lincoln Revealed In His Own Words.* Franklin, TN: Sea Raven Press, 2011; 4) *The Unquotable Abraham Lincoln: The President's Quotes They Don't Want You To Know!* Franklin, TN: Sea Raven Press, 2011.

the humanitarian South—which is why Southern men and women were hard at work trying to solve the many complexities of emancipation when Lincoln invaded Dixie.[16]

Not "traitors." Secession was legal in 1861, and it is still legal today. There is no clause in the Constitution authorizing or forbidding secession. Why? Because it is up to an individual state, not the federal government, to decide whether or not to separate from the Union. It has always been this way and always will—as long as the U.S. Constitution stands. For secession is tacitly guaranteed by the 9th and 10th Amendments, and nothing can change this fact except the destruction of the Bill of rights—the bedrock of the U.S.A.[17]

Not "uncultivated ruffians." The South has always possessed many of the best schools and universities, excellent manners and etiquette, the finest fashions, music, and foods, aesthetic architecture, time-honored American traditions and customs, and among the most patriotic, erudite, ingenious, scholarly, fun-loving, spiritual, and inventive people in the world. In the mid 1800s Dixie was already globally renowned for its hospitality, its sophisticated culture, and its genial people, a reality that holds true to this day.[18]

The Southern Confederacy of the "Civil War" era was made up of a dignified, intense, and strong, but genteel, cultivated, Christian people; one that proved time and time again that it valued freedom above slavery, brotherhood and sisterhood above sectional pride, neighborly love above skin color, and patriotism above politics. You will not find these facts in any mainstream history book (nearly all which are anti-South in nature). But they can be readily ascertained by the reader himself or herself in this very book, for they are overtly reflected in the soulful eyes, traditional clothing, and body language of the men, women, and children pictured on its pages.[19]

CLOSING WORDS

Those with the true knowledge of what happened between April 12, 1861, and April 9, 1865, will view this volume in much the same manner as they do their Bibles; for it is a sacred work, filled with the names and images of a people who valued all that true patriots still hold dear to this day: God, family, tradition, personal freedom, and the U.S. Constitution (with its

---

16. For more on these topics see my book: *Everything You Were Taught About American Slavery War is Wrong, Ask a Southerner!* Spring Hill, TN: Sea Raven Press, 2015.

17. For more on these topics see my book: *All We Ask is to be Let Alone: The Southern Secession Fact Book*. Spring Hill, TN: Sea Raven Press, 2017.

18. For more on these topics see my book: *Everything You Were Taught About the Civil War is Wrong, Ask a Southerner!* 2010. Franklin, TN: Sea Raven Press, revised 2019 ed.

19. For more on these topics see my books: 1) *Rise Up and Call Them Blessed: Victorian Tributes to the Confederate Soldier, 1861-1901*. Spring Hill, TN: Sea Raven Press, 2017; 2) *Victorian Confederate Poetry: The Southern Cause in Verse, 1861-1901*. Spring Hill, TN: Sea Raven Press, 2018; 3) *Confederate Monuments: Why Every American Should Honor Confederate Soldiers and Their Memorials*. Spring Hill, TN: Sea Raven Press, 2018.

assumed guarantee of states' rights).[20]

In arguably the most astounding act of courage recorded in the annals of world history, Southerners made the decision (reluctantly and painfully, it should be strongly noted) to separate from their beloved Union rather than continue to suffer under the tyranny of the Left-wing North. In doing so, the Confederate soldier took up arms to defend a concept: Americanism, or what we now call Conservatism. This makes him the bravest type of man ever known. He marched *toward* the booming of cannon, often barefoot, through ice and snow, acrid gun smoke, and the shrieking of the wounded; he swam *across* rivers of blood; he ran *in the direction* of sheets of hissing lead; he moved *forward* into the face of death as his companions (many of them relatives and lifelong friends) dropped to the ground around him—their bodies torn to pieces by shrapnel, bullet-riddled, drenched in barn-red gore.

One such champion was Confederate Brigadier-General Richard Brook Garnett, who served in Pickett's Division at the Battle of Gettysburg (July 1-July 3, 1863). Approaching the Confederate front, General Garnett hurled his horse straight into the enemy's forward line, as the fog of war and the deafening roar of guns, screams, and cannon enveloped him. This fearless man was never seen again—alive or dead, for later his corpse was picked cleaned by Yankees on the battlefield: after stealing not only his weapons and valuables, but his general's badges as well, his lifeless body was rendered unidentifiable as an officer. His remains thus eventually ended up in an unlocatable Confederate cemetery somewhere in the South with the word "Unknown" engraved upon his headstone.

And herein lies the momentous wonder of the immortal Confederate: he fought and died for an ideal; an ideal that became his cause, the Southern Cause; a cause that was not "lost," as enemies of the truth ignorantly maintain, but which was won on a thousand blood-stained battlefields, and which thrives today stronger than ever before. That cause, the Southern Cause, was Conservatism. My book, *Heroes of the Southern Confederacy*, preserves many of the images of its 19th-Century adherents. The sacred memory of their loyalty, service, and sacrifices will live on for all eternity. For every Confederate man, woman, and child was a hero.

LOCHLAINN SEABROOK
Nashville, Tennessee, USA
April 2021
In Nobis Regnat Christus

---

20. For more on this topic see my books: 1) *Confederacy 101: Amazing Facts You Never Knew About America's Oldest Political Tradition*. Spring Hill, TN: Sea Raven Press, 2015; 2) *Lincoln's War: The Real Cause, the Real Winner, the Real Loser*. Spring Hill, TN: Sea Raven Press, 2016.

Left: Confederate Major-General George Washington Custis Lee (eldest son of General Lee); Center: Southern icon Confederate General Robert Edward Lee; Right: Confederate Lieutenant-Colonel Walter Herron Taylor (General Lee's aide-de-camp). Photo taken circa 1860-1870.

HEROES

of the

SOUTHERN CONFEDERACY

CONFEDERATE OFFICIALS

THE CABINET OF JEFFERSON DAVIS
1861-1865

SIX POSITIONS HELD BY 18 DIFFERENT MEN
All 18 Listed by Position, Name, and Life Span

(FOR MORE INFORMATION ON THE DAVIS CABINET SEE APPENDIX B)

President of the Confederate States of America, Jefferson Davis (1808-1889). "Elected by the Confederate Congress February 9, 1861, receiving the unanimous vote of the six states then composing the Confederacy."

Vice-President of the C.S.A., Alexander Hamilton Stephens (1812-1883).

1. Confederate Secretary of State Robert Augustus Toombs (1810-1885).

2. Confederate Secretary of State Robert Mercer Taliaferro Hunter (1809-1887).

3. Confederate Secretary of State William Montague Browne (1823-1883).

4. Confederate Secretary of the Treasury Christopher Gustav Memminger (1803-1888).

5. Confederate Secretary of the Treasury George Alfred Trenholm (1807-1876).

6. Confederate Secretary of War Leroy Pope Walker (1817-1884).

7. Confederate Secretary of War George Wythe Randolph (1818-1867).

8. Confederate Secretary of War Gustavus Woodson Smith (1821-1896).

9. Confederate Secretary of War James Alexander Seddon (1815-1880).

10. Confederate Secretary of War John Cabell Breckinridge (1821-1875).

11. Confederate Secretary of the Navy Stephen Russell Mallory (1812-1873).

12. Confederate Postmaster General Henry Thomas Ellett (1812-1887).

13. Confederate Postmaster General John Henninger Reagan (1818-1905).

14. Confederate Secretary of State, Attorney General, and Secretary of War Judah Philip Benjamin (1811-1884).

15. Confederate Attorney General Thomas Bragg (1810-1872).

16. Confederate Attorney General Thomas Hill Watts (1819-1892).

17. Confederate Attorney General George Davis (1820-1896).

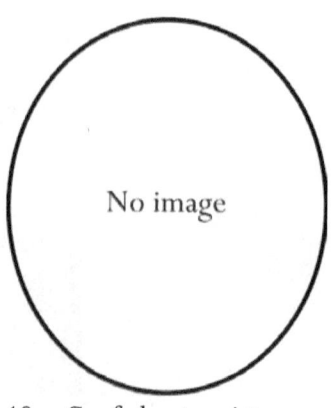

18. Confederate Attorney General Wade Rutledge Keyes (1821-1879).

CONFEDERATE GENERALS

1. Confederate Brigadier-General Daniel Weisiger Adams (1821-1872).

2. Confederate Brigadier-General John Adams (1825-1864).

3. Confederate Brigadier-General William Wirt Adams (1819-1888).

4. Confederate Brigadier-General Edward Porter Alexander (1835-1910).

5. Confederate Brigadier-General Henry Watkins Allen (1820-1866).

6. Confederate Brigadier-General William Wirt Allen (1835-1894).

7. Confederate Brigadier-General George Burgwyn Anderson (1831-1862).

8. Confederate Brigadier-General George Thomas Anderson (1824-1901).

9. Confederate Major-General James Patton Anderson (1822-1872).

10. Confederate Brigadier-General Joseph Reid Anderson (1813-1892).

11. Confederate Lieutenant-General Richard Heron Anderson (1821-1879).

12. Confederate Brigadier-General Robert Houstoun Anderson (1835-1888).

13. Confederate Brigadier-General Samuel Read Anderson (1804-1883).

14. Confederate Brigadier-General James Jay Archer (1817-1864).

15. Confederate Brigadier-General Lewis Addison Armistead (1817-1863).

16. Confederate Brigadier-General Frank Crawford Armstrong (1835-1909).

17. Confederate Brigadier-General Turner Ashby (1828-1862).

18. Confederate Brigadier-General Alpheus Baker (1828-1891).

19. Confederate Brigadier-General Laurence Simmons Baker (1830-1907).

20. Confederate Brigadier-General William Edwin Baldwin (1827-1864).

21. Confederate Brigadier-General William Barksdale (1821-1863).

22. Confederate Brigadier-General Rufus Barringer (1821-1895).

23. Confederate Brigadier-General John Decatur Barry (1839-1867).

24. Confederate Brigadier-General Seth Maxwell Barton (1829-1900).

25. Confederate Major-General William Brimage Bate (1826-1905).

26. Confederate Brigadier-General Cullen Andrews Battle (1829-1905).

27. Confederate Brigadier-General Richard Lee Turberville Beale (1819-1893).

28. Confederate Brigadier-General William Nelson Rector Beall (1825-1883).

29. Confederate General Pierre Gustave Toutant Beauregard (1818-1893).

30. Confederate Brigadier-General Barnard Elliott Bee (1824-1861).

31. Confederate Brigadier-General Hamilton Prioleau Bee (1822-1897).

32. Confederate Brigadier-General Tyree Harris Bell (1815-1902).

33. Confederate Brigadier-General Henry Lewis Benning (1814-1875).

34. Confederate Brigadier-General Samuel Benton (1820-1864).

35. Confederate Brigadier-General Albert Gallatin Blanchard (1810-1891).

36. Confederate Brigadier-General William Robertson Boggs (1829-1911).

37. Confederate Brigadier-General Milledge Luke Bonham (1813-1890).

38. Confederate Major-General John Stevens Bowen (1830-1863).

39. Confederate General Braxton Bragg (1817-1876).

40. Confederate Brigadier-General Lawrence O'Bryan Branch (1820-1862).

41. Confederate Brigadier-General William Lindsay Brandon (circa 1800-1890).

42. Confederate Brigadier-General William Felix Brantley (1830-1870).

43. Confederate Brigadier-General John Bratton (1831-1898).

44. Confederate Major-General John Cabell Breckinridge (1821-1875).

45. Confederate Brigadier-General Theodore Washington Brevard (1835-1882).

46. Confederate Major-General John Calvin Brown (1827-1889).

47. Confederate Brigadier-General William Montague Browne (1823-1883).

48. Confederate Brigadier-General Goode Bryan (1811-1885).

49. Confederate Lieutenant-General Simon Bolivar Buckner (1823-1914).

50. Confederate Brigadier-General Abraham Buford (1820-1884).

51. Confederate Brigadier-General Michael Jefferson Bulger (1806-1900).

52. Confederate Brigadier-General Robert Bullock (1828-1905).

53. Confederate Major-General Matthew Calbraith Butler (1836-1909).

54. Confederate Brigadier-General William Lewis Cabell (1827-1911).

55. Confederate Brigadier-General Alexander William Campbell (1828-1893).

56. Confederate Brigadier-General James Cantey (1818-1874).

57. Confederate Brigadier-General Ellison Capers (1837-1908).

58. Confederate Brigadier-General William Henry Carroll (1810-1868).

59. Confederate Brigadier-General John Carpenter Carter (1837-1864).

60. Confederate Brigadier-General James Ronald Chalmers (1831-1898).

61. Confederate Brigadier-General John Randolph Chambliss Jr. (1833-1864).

62. Confederate Major-General Benjamin Franklin Cheatham (1820-1886).

63. Confederate Brigadier-General James Chesnut Jr. (1815-1885).

64. Confederate Brigadier-General Robert Hall Chilton (1815-1879).

65. Confederate Major-General Thomas James Churchill (1824-1905).

66. Confederate Brigadier-General James Holt Clanton (1827-1871).

67. Confederate Brigadier-General Charles Clark (1811-1877).

68. Confederate Brigadier-General John Bullock Clark Jr. (1831-1885).

69. Confederate Major-General Henry DeLamar Clayton (1827-1889).

70. Confederate Major-General Patrick Ronayne Cleburne (1828-1864).

71. Confederate Brigadier-General Thomas Lanier Clingman (1812-1897).

72. Confederate Major-General Howell Cobb (1815-1868).

73. Confederate Brigadier-General Thomas Reade Rootes Cobb (1823-1862).

74. Confederate Brigadier-General Philip St. George Cocke (1809-1861).

75. Confederate Brigadier-General Francis Marion Cockrell (1834-1915).

76. Confederate Brigadier-General Alfred Holt Colquitt (1824-1894).

77. Confederate Brigadier-General Raleigh Edward Colston (1825-1896).

78. Confederate Brigadier-General James Connor (1829-1883).

79. Confederate Brigadier-General Philip Cook (1817-1894).

80. Confederate Brigadier-General John Rogers Cooke (1833-1891).

81. Confederate Brigadier-General Douglas Hancock Cooper (1815-1879).

82. Confederate General Samuel Cooper (1798-1876).

83. Confederate Brigadier-General Montgomery Dent Corse (1816-1895).

84. Confederate Brigadier-General George Blake Cosby (1830-1909).

85. Confederate Brigadier-General William Ruffin Cox (1832-1919).

86. Confederate Major-General George Bibb Crittenden (1812-1880).

87. Confederate Brigadier-General Alfred Cumming (1829-1910).

88. Confederate Brigadier-General Junius Daniel (1828-1864).

89. Confederate Brigadier-General Henry Brevard Davidson (1831-1899).

90. Confederate Brigadier-General Joseph Robert Davis (1825-1896).

91. Confederate Major-General Reuben Davis (1813-1890).

92. Confederate Brigadier-General William George Mackey Davis (1812-1898).

93. Confederate Brigadier-General James Dearing (1840-1865).

94. Confederate Brigadier-General Zachariah Cantey Deas (1819-1882).

95. Confederate Brigadier-General Julius Adolph de Lagnel (1827-1912).

96. Confederate Brigadier-General James Deshler (1833-1863).

97. Confederate Brigadier-General George Gibbs Dibrell (1822-1888).

98. Confederate Brigadier-General Thomas Pleasant Dockery (1833-1898).

99. Confederate Brigadier-General George Pierce Doles (1830-1864).

100. Confederate Major-General Daniel Smith Donelson (1825-1863).

101. Confederate Brigadier-General Thomas Fenwick Drayton (1808-1891).

102. Confederate Brigadier-General Dudley McIver DuBose (1834-1883).

103. Confederate Brigadier-General Basil Wilson Duke (1838-1916).

104. Confederate Brigadier-General Johnson Kelly Duncan (1827-1862).

105. Confederate Brigadier-General John Dunovant (1825-1864).

106. Confederate Lieutenant-General Jubal Anderson Early (1816-1894).

107. Confederate Brigadier-General John Echols (1823-1896).

108. Confederate Brigadier-General Matthew Duncan Ector (1822-1879).

109. Confederate Brigadier-General Stephen Elliott Jr. (1830-1866).

110. Confederate Major-General Arnold Elzey (1816-1871).

111. Confederate Brigadier-General Clement Anselm Evans (1833-1911).

112. Confederate Brigadier-General Nathan George Evans (1824-1868).

113. Confederate Lieutenant-General Richard Stoddert Ewell (1817-1872).

114. Confederate Major-General James Fleming Fagan (1828-1893).

115. Confederate Brigadier-General Thomas Turner Fauntleroy (1795-1883).

116. Confederate Brigadier-General Winfield Scott Featherston (1820-1891).

117. Confederate Major-General Samuel Wragg Ferguson (1834-1917).

118. Confederate Major-General Charles William Field (1828-1892).

119. Confederate Brigadier-General Joseph J. Finegan (1814-1885).

120. Confederate Brigadier-General Jesse Johnson Finley (1812-1904).

121. Confederate Major-General John Buchanan Floyd (1806-1863).

122. Confederate Major-General John Horace Forney (1829-1902).

123. Confederate Brigadier-General William Henry Forney (1823-1894).

124. Confederate Lieutenant-General Nathan Bedford Forrest (1821-1877).

125. Confederate Brigadier-General John Wesley Frazer (1827-1906).

126. Confederate Major-General Samuel Gibbs French (1818-1910).

127. Confederate Brigadier-General Daniel Marsh Frost (1823-1900).

128. Confederate Brigadier-General Birkett Davenport Fry (1822-1891).

129. Confederate Brigadier-General Richard Montgomery Gano (1830-1913).

130. Confederate Major-General Franklin Gardner (1823-1873).

131. Confederate Brigadier-General William Montgomery Gardner (1824-1901).

132. Confederate Brigadier-General Samuel Garland Jr. (1830-1862).

133. Confederate Brigadier-General Richard Brooke Garnett (1817-1863).

134. Confederate Brigadier-General Robert Selden Garnett (1819-1861).

135. Confederate Brigadier-General Isham Warren Garrott (1816-1863).

136. Confederate Brigadier-General Lucius Jeremiah Gartrell (1821-1891).

137. Confederate Brigadier-General Martin Witherspoon Gary (1831-1881).

138. Confederate Brigadier-General Richard Caswell Gatlin (1809-1896).

139. Confederate Brigadier-General Samuel Jameson Gholson (1808-1883).

140. Confederate Brigadier-General Randall Lee Gibson (1832-1892).

141. Confederate Major-General Jeremy Francis Gilmer (1818-1883).

142. Confederate Brigadier-General Victor Jean Baptiste Girardey (1837-1864).

143. Confederate Brigadier-General States Rights Gist (1831-1864).

144. Confederate Brigadier-General Adley Hogan Gladden (1810-1862).

145. Confederate Brigadier-General Archibald Campbell Godwin (1831-1864).

146. Confederate Brigadier-General James Monroe Goggin (1820-1889).

147. Confederate Brigadier-General George Washington Gordon (1836-1911).

148. Confederate Brigadier-General James Byron Gordon (1822-1864).

149. Confederate Major-General John Brown Gordon (1832-1904).

150. Confederate Brigadier-General Josiah Gorgas (1818-1883).

151. Confederate Brigadier-General Daniel Chevillette Govan (1827-1911).

152. Confederate Brigadier-General Archibald Gracie Jr. (1832-1864).

153. Confederate Brigadier-General Hiram Bronson Granbury (1831-1864).

154. Confederate Brigadier-General Henry Gray (1816-1892).

155. Confederate Brigadier-General John Breckinridge Grayson (1806-1861).

156. Confederate Brigadier-General Martin Edwin Green (1815-1863).

157. Confederate Major-General Thomas Green (1814-1864).

158. Confederate Brigadier-General Elkanah Brackin Greer (1825-1877).

159. Confederate Brigadier-General John Gregg (1828-1864).

160. Confederate Brigadier-General Maxcy Gregg (1814-1862).

161. Confederate Brigadier-General Richard Griffith (1814-1862).

162. Confederate Major-General Bryan Grimes (1828-1880).

163. Confederate Acting Brigadier-General James Hagan (1822-1901).

164. Confederate Brigadier-General Johnson Hagood (1829-1898).

165. Confederate Lieutenant-General Wade Hampton (1818-1902).

166. Confederate Brigadier-General Roger Weightman Hanson (1827-1863).

167. Confederate Lieutenant-General William Joseph Hardee (1815-1873).

168. Confederate Brigadier-General William Polk Hardeman (1816-1898).

169. Confederate Brigadier-General Nathaniel Harrison Harris (1834-1900).

170. Confederate Brigadier-General James Edward Harrison (1815-1875).

171. Confederate Brigadier-General Thomas Harrison (1823-1891).

172. Confederate Brigadier-General Robert Hopkins Hatton (1826-1862).

173. Confederate Brigadier-General James Morrison Hawes (1824-1889).

174. Confederate Brigadier-General Alexander Travis Hawthorn (1825-1899).

175. Confederate Major-General Harry Thompson Hays (1820-1876).

176. Confederate Brigadier-General Louis Hébert (1820-1901).

177. Confederate Brigadier-General Paul Octave Hébert (1818-1880).

178. Confederate Brigadier-General Benjamin Hardin Helm (1831-1863).

179. Confederate Brigadier-General Henry Heth (1825-1899).

180. Confederate Brigadier-General Edward Higgins (1821-1875).

181. Confederate Lieutenant-General Ambrose Powell Hill (1825-1865).

182. Confederate Brigadier-General Benjamin Jefferson Hill (1825-1880).

183. Confederate Lieutenant-General Daniel Harvey Hill (1821-1889).

184. Confederate Major-General Thomas Carmichael Hindman Jr. (1828-1868).

185. Confederate Brigadier-General George Baird Hodge (1828-1892).

186. Confederate Brigadier-General Joseph Lewis Hogg (1806-1862).

187. Confederate Major-General Robert Frederick Hoke (1837-1912).

188. Confederate Lieutenant-General Theophilus Hunter Holmes (1804-1880).

189. Confederate Brigadier-General James Thadeus Holtzclaw (1833-1893).

190. Confederate General John Bell Hood (1831-1879).

191. Confederate Major-General Benjamin Huger (1805-1877).

192. Confederate Brigadier-General William Young Conn Humes (1830-1882).

193. Confederate Brigadier-General Benjamin Grubb Humphreys (1808-1882).

194. Confederate Brigadier-General Eppa Hunton (1822-1908).

195. Confederate Brigadier-General John Daniel Imboden (1823-1895).

196. Confederate Brigadier-General Alfred Iverson Jr. (1829-1911).

197. Confederate Brigadier-General Alfred Eugene Jackson (1807-1889).

198. Confederate Brigadier-General Henry Rootes Jackson (1820-1898).

199. Confederate Brigadier-General John King Jackson (1828-1866).

200. Confederate Lieutenant-General Thomas Jonathan Jackson (1824-1863).

201. Confederate Brigadier-General William Hicks Jackson (1835-1903).

202. Confederate Brigadier-General William Lowther Jackson (1825-1890).

203. Confederate Brigadier-General Albert Gallatin Jenkins (1830-1864).

204. Confederate Brigadier-General Micah Jenkins (1835-1864).

205. Confederate Brigadier-General Adam Rankin Johnson (1834-1922).

206. Confederate Brigadier-General Bradley Tyler Johnson (1829-1903).

207. Confederate Major-General Bushrod Rust Johnson (1817-1880).

208. Confederate Major-General Edward Johnson (1816-1873).

209. Confederate General Albert Sidney Johnston (1803-1862).

210. Confederate Brigadier-General George Doherty Johnston (1832-1910).

211. Confederate General Joseph Eggleston Johnston (1807-1891).

212. Confederate Brigadier-General Robert Daniel Johnston (1837-1919).

213. Confederate Major-General David Rumph Jones (1825-1863).

214. Confederate Brigadier-General John Marshall Jones (1820-1864).

215. Confederate Brigadier-General John Robert Jones (1827-1901).

216. Confederate Major-General Samuel Jones (1819-1887).

217. Confederate Brigadier-General William Edmondson Jones (1824-1864).

218. Confederate Brigadier-General Thomas Jordan (1819-1895).

219. Confederate Brigadier-General John Herbert Kelly (1840-1864).

220. Confederate Major-General James Lawson Kemper (1823-1895).

221. Confederate Brigadier-General John Doby Kennedy (1840-1896).

222. Confederate Major-General Joseph Brevard Kershaw (1822-1894).

223. Confederate Brigadier-General William Whedbee Kirkland (1833-1915).

224. Confederate Brigadier-General James Henry Lane (1833-1907).

225. Confederate Brigadier-General Walter Paye Lane (1817-1892).

226. Confederate Brigadier-General Evander McIvor Law (1836-1920).

227. Confederate Brigadier-General Alexander Robert Lawton (1818-1896).

228. Confederate Brigadier-General Danville Leadbetter (1811-1866).

229. Confederate Brigadier-General Edwin Gray Lee (1836-1870).

230. Confederate Major-General Fitzhugh Lee (1835-1905).

231. Confederate Major-General George Washington Custis Lee (1832-1913).

232. Confederate General, as well as General-in-Chief of the Armies of the Confederate States of America, Robert Edward Lee (1807-1870).

233. Confederate Lieutenant-General Stephen Dill Lee (1833-1908).

234. Confederate Major-General William Henry Fitzhugh Lee (1837-1891).

235. Confederate Brigadier-General Collett Leventhorpe (1815-1889).

236. Confederate Brigadier-General Joseph Horace Lewis (1824-1904).

237. Confederate Brigadier-General William Gaston Lewis (1835-1901).

238. Confederate Brigadier-General St. John Richardson Liddell (1815-1870).

239. Confederate Brigadier-General Robert Doak Lilley (1836-1886).

240. Confederate Brigadier-General Lewis Henry Little (1817-1862).

241. Confederate Brigadier-General Thomas Muldrup Logan (1840-1914).

242. Confederate Major-General Lunsford Lindsay Lomax (1835-1913).

243. Confederate Brigadier-General Armistead Lindsay Long (1825-1891).

244. Confederate Lieutenant-General James Longstreet (1821-1904).

245. Confederate Major-General William Wing Loring (1818-1886).

246. Confederate Major-General Mansfield Lovell (1822-1884).

247. Confederate Brigadier-General Mark Perrin Lowrey (1828-1885).

248. Confederate Brigadier-General Robert Lowry (1829-1910).

249. Confederate Brigadier-General Hylan Benton Lyon (1836-1907).

250. Confederate Brigadier-General William Whann Mackall (1817-1891).

251. Confederate Brigadier-General William MacRae (1834-1882).

252. Confederate Brigadier-General John Bankhead Magruder (1807-1871).

253. Confederate Major-General William Mahone (1826-1895).

254. Confederate Brigadier-General James Patrick Major (1836-1877).

255. Confederate Brigadier-General George Earl Maney (1826-1901).

256. Confederate Brigadier-General Arthur Middleton Manigault (1824-1886).

257. Confederate Major-General John Sappington Marmaduke (1833-1887).

258. Confederate Brigadier-General Humphrey Marshall (1812-1872).

259. Confederate Major-General James Green Martin (1819-1878).

260. Confederate Major-General William Thompson Martin (1823-1910).

261. Confederate Major-General Dabney Herndon Maury (1822-1900).

262. Confederate Major-General Samuel Bell Maxey (1825-1895).

263. Confederate Brigadier-General John McCausland (1836-1927).

264. Confederate Brigadier-General William McComb (1828-1918).

265. Confederate Major-General John Porter McCown (1815-1879).

266. Confederate Brigadier-General Benjamin McCulloch (1811-1862).

267. Confederate Brigadier-General Henry Eustace McCulloch (1816-1895).

268. Confederate Brigadier-General Samuel McGowan (1819-1897).

269. Confederate Brigadier-General James McQueen McIntosh (1828-1862).

270. Confederate Major-General Lafayette McLaws (1821-1897).

271. Confederate Brigadier-General Evander McNair (1820-1902).

272. Confederate Brigadier-General Dandridge McRae (1829-1899).

273. Confederate Brigadier-General Hugh Weedon Mercer (1808-1877).

274. Confederate Brigadier-General William Miller (1820-1909).

275. Confederate Brigadier-General Young Marshall Moody (1822-1866).

276. Confederate Brigadier-General John Creed Moore (1824-1910).

277. Confederate Brigadier-General Patrick Theodore Moore (1821-1883).

278. Confederate Brigadier-General John Hunt Morgan (1825-1864).

279. Confederate Brigadier-General John Tyler Morgan (1824-1907).

280. Confederate Brigadier-General Jean Jacques Alfred Alexander Mouton (1829-1864).

281. Confederate Brigadier-General Allison Nelson (1822-1862).

282. Confederate Brigadier-General Francis Redding Tillou Nicholls (1834-1912).

283. Confederate Brigadier-General Lucius Bellinger Northrop (1811-1894).

284. Confederate Brigadier-General Edward Asbury O'Neal (1818-1890).

285. Confederate Brigadier-General Richard Lucian Page (1807-1901).

286. Confederate Brigadier-General Joseph Benjamin Palmer (1825-1890).

287. Confederate Brigadier-General Mosby Monroe Parsons (1822-1865).

288. Confederate Brigadier-General Elisha Franklin Paxton (1828-1863).

289. Confederate Brigadier-General William Henry Fitzhugh Payne (1830-1904).

290. Confederate Brigadier-General William Raine Peck (1818-1871).

291. Confederate Brigadier-General John Pegram (1832-1865).

292. Confederate Lieutenant-General John Clifford Pemberton (1814-1881).

293. Confederate Major-General William Dorsey Pender (1834-1863).

294. Confederate Brigadier-General William Nelson Pendleton (1809-1883).

295. Confederate Brigadier-General Abner Monroe Perrin (1827-1864).

296. Confederate Brigadier-General Edward Aylesworth Perry (1831-1889).

297. Confederate Brigadier-General William Flank Perry (1823-1901).

298. Confederate Brigadier-General James Johnston Pettigrew (1828-1863).

299. Confederate Brigadier-General Edmund Winston Pettus (1821-1907).

300. Confederate Major-General George Edward Pickett (1825-1875).

301. Confederate Brigadier-General Albert Pike (1809-1891).

302. Confederate Brigadier-General Gideon Johnson Pillow (1806-1878).

303. Confederate Major-General Camille Armand Jules Marie, Prince de Polignac (1832-1913).

304. Confederate Lieutenant-General Leonidas Polk (1806-1864).

305. Confederate Brigadier-General Lucius Eugene Polk (1833-1892).

306. Confederate Brigadier-General Carnot Posey (1818-1863).

307. Confederate Brigadier-General John Smith Preston (1809-1881).

308. Confederate Major-General William Preston (1816-1887).

309. Confederate Major-General Sterling Price (1809-1867).

310. Confederate Brigadier-General Roger Atkinson Pryor (1828-1919).

311. Confederate Brigadier-General William Andrew Quarles (1825-1893).

312. Confederate Brigadier-General Gabriel James Rains (1803-1881).

313. Confederate Brigadier-General James Edwards Rains (1833-1862).

314. Confederate Major General Stephen Dodson Ramseur (1837-1864).

315. Confederate Brigadier-General George Wythe Randolph (1818-1867).

316. Confederate Brigadier-General Matt Whitaker Ransom (1826-1904).

317. Confederate Major-General Robert Ransom Jr. (1828-1892).

318. Confederate Brigadier-General Alexander Welch Reynolds (1816-1876).

319. Confederate Brigadier-General Daniel Harris Reynolds (1832-1902).

320. Confederate Brigadier-General Robert Vinkler Richardson (1820-1870).

321. Confederate Brigadier-General Roswell Sabine Ripley (1823-1887).

322. Confederate Brigadier-General John Selden Roane (1817-1867).

323. Confederate Brigadier-General William Paul Roberts (1841-1910).

324. Confederate Brigadier-General Beverly Holcombe Robertson (1827-1910).

325. Confederate Brigadier-General Felix Huston Robertson (1839-1928).

326. Confederate Brigadier-General Jerome Bonaparte Robertson (1815-1891).

327. Confederate Brigadier-General Philip Dale Roddey (1826-1897).

328. Confederate Major-General Robert Emmett Rodes (1829-1864).

329. Confederate Brigadier-General Lawrence Sullivan Ross (1838-1898).

330. Confederate Major-General Thomas Lafayette Rosser (1836-1910).

331. Confederate Brigadier-General Edmund Winchester Rucker (1835-1924).

332. Confederate Brigadier-General Daniel Ruggles (1810-1897).

333. Confederate Brigadier-General Albert Rust (1818-1870).

334. Confederate Brigadier-General Isaac Munroe St. John (1827-1880).

335. Confederate Brigadier-General John Caldwell Calhoun Sanders (1840-1864).

336. Confederate Brigadier-General Alfred Moore Scales (1827-1892).

337. Confederate Brigadier-General Thomas Moore Scott (1829-1876).

338. Confederate Brigadier-General William Read Scurry (1821-1864).

339. Confederate Brigadier-General Claudius Wistar Sears (1817-1891).

340. Confederate Brigadier-General Paul Jones Semmes (1815-1863).

341. Confederate Brigadier-General Jacob Hunter Sharp (1833-1907).

342. Confederate Brigadier-General Joseph Orville Shelby (1830-1897).

343. Confederate Brigadier-General Charles Miller Shelley (1833-1907).

344. Confederate Brigadier-General Francis Asbury Shoup (1834-1896).

345. Confederate Brigadier-General Henry Hopkins Sibley (1816-1886).

346. Confederate Brigadier-General James Phillip Simms (1837-1887).

347. Confederate Brigadier-General William Yarnel Slack (1816-1862).

348. Confederate Brigadier-General James Edwin Slaughter (1827-1901).

349. Confederate General Edmund Kirby Smith (1824-1893).

350. Confederate Major-General Gustavus Woodson Smith (1821-1896).

351. Confederate Brigadier-General James Argyle Smith (1831-1901).

352. Confederate Major-General Martin Luther Smith (1819-1866).

353. Confederate Brigadier-General Preston Smith (1823-1863).

354. Confederate Brigadier-General Thomas Benton Smith (1838-1923).

355. Confederate Major-General William Smith (1797-1887).

356. Confederate Brigadier-General William Duncan Smith (1825-1862).

357. Confederate Brigadier-General Gilbert Moxley Sorrel (1838-1901).

358. Confederate Brigadier-General Leroy Augustus Stafford (1822-1864).

359. Confederate Brigadier-General Peter Burwell Starke (1815-1888).

360. Confederate Brigadier-General William Edwin Starke (1814-1862).

361. Confederate Brigadier-General William Steele (1819-1885).

362. Confederate Brigadier-General George Hume Steuart (1828-1903).

363. Confederate Brigadier-General Clement Hoffman Stevens (1821-1864).

364. Confederate Brigadier-General Walter Husted Stevens (1827-1867).

365. Confederate Major-General Carter Littlepage Stevenson (1817-1888).

366. Confederate Lieutenant-General Alexander Peter Stewart (1821-1908).

367. Confederate Brigadier-General Marcellus Augustus Stovall (1818-1895).

368. Confederate Brigadier-General Otho French Strahl (1831-1864).

369. Confederate Major-General James Ewell Brown Stuart (1833-1864).

370. Confederate Major-General William Booth Taliaferro (1822-1898).

371. Confederate Brigadier-General James Camp Tappan (1825-1906).

372. Confederate Lieutenant-General Richard Taylor (1826-1879).

373. Confederate Brigadier-General Thomas Hart Taylor (1825-1901).

374. Confederate Brigadier-General James Barbour Terrill (1838-1864).

375. Confederate Brigadier-General William Terry (1824-1888).

376. Confederate Brigadier-General William Richard Terry (1827-1897).

377. Confederate Brigadier-General Allen Thomas (1830-1907).

378. Confederate Brigadier-General Bryan Morel Thomas (1836-1905).

379. Confederate Brigadier-General Edward Lloyd Thomas (1825-1898).

380. Confederate Brigadier-General Lloyd Tilghman (1816-1863).

381. Confederate Brigadier-General Robert Augustus Toombs (1810-1885).

382. Confederate Brigadier-General Thomas Fentress Toon (1840-1902).

383. Confederate Brigadier-General Edward Dorr Tracy (1833-1863).

384. Confederate Brigadier-General James Heyward Trapier (1815-1865).

385. Confederate Brigadier-General Isaac Ridgeway Trimble (1802-1888).

386. Confederate Brigadier-General William Feimster Tucker (1827-1881).

387. Confederate Major-General David Emmanuel Twiggs (1790-1862).

388. Confederate Brigadier-General Robert Charles Tyler (circa 1833-1865).

389. Confederate Brigadier-General Robert Brank Vance (1828-1899).

390. Confederate Major-General Earl Van Dorn (1820-1863).

391. Confederate Brigadier-General Alfred Jefferson Vaughan Jr. (1830-1899).

392. Confederate Brigadier-General John Crawford Vaughn (1824-1875).

393. Confederate Brigadier-General John Bordenave Villepigue (1830-1862).

394. Confederate Brigadier-General Henry Harrison Walker (1832-1912).

395. Confederate Brigadier-General James Alexander Walker (1832-1901).

396. Confederate Major-General John George Walker (1822-1893).

397. Confederate Brigadier-General Leroy Pope Walker (1817-1884).

398. Confederate Brigadier-General Lucius Marshall Walker (1829-1863).

399. Confederate Brigadier-General Reuben Lindsay Walker (1827-1890).

400. Confederate Major-General William Henry Talbot Walker (1816-1864).

401. Confederate Brigadier-General William Stephen Walker (1822-1899).

402. Confederate Brigadier-General William Henry Wallace (1827-1901).

403. Confederate Major-General Edward Cary Walthall (1831-1898).

404. Confederate Brigadier-General Richard Waterhouse Jr. (1832-1876).

405. Confederate Brigadier-General Stand Watie (1806-1871).

406. Confederate Brigadier-General Thomas Neville Waul (1813-1903).

407. Confederate Brigadier-General Henry Constantine Wayne (1815-1883).

408. Confederate Brigadier-General David Addison Weisiger (1818-1899).

409. Confederate Brigadier-General Gabriel Colvin Wharton (1824-1906).

410. Confederate Major-General John Austin Wharton (1828-1865).

411. Confederate Major-General Joseph Wheeler (1836-1906).

412. Confederate Brigadier-General John Wilkins Whitfield (1818-1879).

413. Confederate Brigadier-General William Henry Chase Whiting (1824-1865).

414. Confederate Brigadier-General Williams Carter Wickham (1820-1888).

415. Confederate Brigadier-General Louis Trezevant Wigfall (1816-1874).

416. Confederate Major-General Cadmus Marcellus Wilcox (1824-1890).

417. Confederate Brigadier-General John Stuart Williams (1818-1898).

418. Confederate Brigadier-General Claudius Charles Wilson (1831-1863).

419. Confederate Brigadier-General Charles Sidney Winder (1829-1862).

420. Confederate Brigadier-General John Henry Winder (1800-1865).

421. Confederate Brigadier-General Henry Alexander Wise (1806-1876).

422. Confederate Major-General Jones Mitchell Withers (1814-1890).

423. Confederate Brigadier-General William Tatum Wofford (1824-1884).

424. Confederate Brigadier-General Sterling Alexander Martin Wood (1823-1891).

425. Confederate Major-General Ambrose Ransom Wright (1826-1872).

426. Confederate Brigadier-General Marcus Joseph Wright (1831-1922).

427. Confederate Brigadier-General Zebulon York (1819-1900).

428. Confederate Major-General Pierce Manning Butler Young (1836-1896).

429. Confederate Brigadier-General William Hugh Young (1838-1901).

430. Confederate Brigadier-General Felix Kirk Zollicoffer (1812-1862).

CONFEDERATE SOLDIERS & CIVILIANS

Confederate soldier Jonathan Sweet, circa 1861-1865.

Confederate soldier, identity unknown, circa 1861-1865.

Confederate soldier, identity unknown, circa 1861-1865.

Confederate Captain Augustus C. Thompson, circa 1861-1863.

Confederate soldier, identity unknown, circa 1861-1865.

Confederate soldier, E. F. Powell, circa 1861-1865.

Confederate soldier, identity unknown, circa 1861-1865.

Confederate soldier, identity unknown, prisoner of war at Camp Douglas, Illinois, circa 1861-1865.

Confederate widow and child in mourning, identity unknown (she may be Mrs. James Shields). She is wearing a brooch bearing an image of what is probably her deceased husband.

Confederate soldier, identity unknown, circa 1861-1865.

Confederate soldier (right), identity unknown, possibly with his father (left), circa 1861-1865.

Confederate Chaplain Thomas Nelson, 1864.

Possibly Confederate Captain Warner Griffith Welsh (left) and Confederate Lieutenant William H. B. Dorsey (right), circa 1861-1865.

Confederate soldier, identity unknown, circa 1861-1865.

Confederate soldier, identity unknown, circa 1861-1865.

Confederate soldier, identity unknown, 1861.

Confederate soldier, identity unknown, circa 1861-1865.

Confederate soldier, identity unknown, circa 1861-1865.

Confederate soldier, identity unknown, circa 1861-1865.

Wife of Confederate soldier to the left, identity unknown, circa 1861-1865.

Confederate soldier, identity unknown, circa 1861-1865.

Confederate soldier, identity unknown, circa 1861-1865.

Confederate soldier, identity unknown, circa 1861-1865.

Confederate soldier, identity unknown, circa 1861-1865.

Confederate soldier, identity unknown, circa 1861-1865.

Confederate soldier, identity unknown, circa 1861-1865.

Confederate soldier, identity unknown, circa 1861-1865.

Confederate soldiers, identities unknown, circa 1861-1865.

Confederate soldier, identity unknown, circa 1861-1865.

Confederate soldier, identity unknown, circa 1861-1865.

Confederate soldier, identity unknown, circa 1861-1865.

Confederate soldiers, identities unknown, circa 1861-1865.

Confederate soldier, identity unknown, circa 1861-1865.

Wife of Confederate soldier to the left, identity unknown, circa 1861-1865.

Confederate soldier, identity unknown, circa 1861-1865.

Confederate soldier, identity unknown, circa 1861-1865.

Confederate soldier, identity unknown, circa 1861-1865.

Confederate soldier, identity unknown, circa 1861-1865.

Confederate soldier, identity unknown, circa 1861-1865.

Confederate soldier, identity unknown, circa 1861-1865.

Confederate soldier, identity unknown, circa 1861-1865.

Confederate soldier, identity unknown, circa 1861-1865.

Confederate soldier, identity unknown, circa 1861-1865.

Confederate woman, identity unknown; probably the wife of Confederate soldier to the left, circa 1861-1865.

Confederate soldier, identity unknown, circa 1861-1865.

Confederate soldier, identity unknown, circa 1861-1865.

Confederate soldier, identity unknown, circa 1861-1865.

Confederate soldier, identity unknown, circa 1861-1865.

Confederate soldier, identity unknown, circa 1861-1865.

Confederate soldier, identity unknown, circa 1861-1865.

Confederate soldier, identity unknown, circa 1861-1865.

Confederate soldier, identity unknown, circa 1861-1865.

Confederate soldier, identity unknown, circa 1861-1865.

Confederate soldier, identity unknown, circa 1861-1865.

Confederate soldier, identity unknown, circa 1861-1865.

Confederate soldier, identity unknown, circa 1861-1865.

Confederate soldier, identity unknown, circa 1861-1865.

Confederate soldier, identity unknown, circa 1861-1865.

Confederate soldier, identity unknown, circa 1861-1865.

Confederate soldier, identity unknown, circa 1861-1865.

Confederate soldier, identity unknown, circa 1861-1865.

Confederate soldier and his wife, identities unknown, circa 1861-1865.

Confederate soldier, identity unknown, circa 1861-1865.

Confederate soldier, identity unknown, circa 1861-1865.

Confederate soldiers, identities unknown, circa 1861-1865.

Confederate soldier, identity unknown, circa 1861-1865.

Confederate soldier, identity unknown, circa 1861-1865.

Confederate soldier, identity unknown, circa 1861-1865.

Confederate soldier, identity unknown, circa 1861-1865.

Confederate soldier, identity unknown, circa 1861-1865.

Confederate soldier, identity unknown, circa 1861-1865.

Confederate soldier, identity unknown, circa 1861-1865.

Confederate soldier, identity unknown, circa 1861-1865.

Confederate soldier, identity unknown, circa 1861-1865.

Confederate soldier, identity unknown, circa 1861-1865.

Confederate soldier, identity unknown, circa 1861-1865.

Confederate soldier, identity unknown, circa 1861-1865.

Confederate soldier, identity unknown, circa 1861-1865.

Confederate soldier, identity unknown, circa 1861-1865.

Confederate soldier, identity unknown, circa 1861-1865.

Confederate soldier, identity unknown, circa 1861-1865.

Confederate soldier, identity unknown, circa 1861-1865.

Confederate soldier, identity unknown, circa 1861-1865.

Confederate soldier, identity unknown, circa 1861-1865.

Confederate soldier, identity unknown, circa 1861-1865.

Confederate soldier, identity unknown, circa 1861-1865.

Confederate soldier, identity unknown, circa 1861-1865.

Confederate soldier, identity unknown, circa 1861-1865.

Confederate soldier, identity unknown, circa 1861-1865.

Confederate soldier, identity unknown, circa 1861-1865.

Confederate soldier, identity unknown, circa 1861-1865.

Confederate soldier, identity unknown, circa 1861-1865.

Confederate soldier, identity unknown, circa 1861-1865.

Confederate soldier, identity unknown, circa 1861-1865.

Confederate soldier, identity unknown, circa 1861-1865.

Confederate soldier, identity unknown, circa 1861-1865.

Confederate soldier, identity unknown, circa 1861-1865.

Confederate soldiers, identities unknown, circa 1861-1865.

Confederate soldier, identity unknown, circa 1861-1865.

Confederate soldier, identity unknown, circa 1861-1865.

Confederate soldier, identity unknown, circa 1861-1865.

Confederate soldier, identity unknown, circa 1861-1865.

Confederate soldier, identity unknown, circa 1861-1865.

Confederate soldier, identity unknown, circa 1861-1865.

Confederate soldiers, identities unknown, circa 1861-1865.

Confederate soldier, identity unknown, circa 1861-1865.

Confederate soldier, identity unknown, circa 1861-1865.

Confederate soldier, identity unknown, circa 1861-1865.

Confederate soldier, identity unknown, circa 1861-1865.

Confederate soldier, identity unknown, circa 1861-1865.

Confederate soldiers, identities unknown, circa 1861-1865.

Confederate soldier, identity unknown, circa 1861-1865.

Confederate soldier, identity unknown, circa 1861-1865.

Confederate soldier, identity unknown, circa 1861-1865.

Confederate soldier, identity unknown, circa 1861-1865.

Confederate soldier, identity unknown, circa 1861-1865.

Confederate soldier, identity unknown, circa 1861-1865.

Confederate soldier, identity unknown, circa 1861-1865.

Confederate soldier, identity unknown, circa 1861-1865.

Confederate soldier, identity unknown, circa 1861-1865.

Confederate soldier, identity unknown, circa 1861-1865.

Confederate soldier, identity unknown, circa 1861-1865.

Confederate soldier, identity unknown, circa 1861-1865.

Confederate soldier, identity unknown, circa 1861-1865.

Confederate soldier, identity unknown, circa 1861-1865.

Confederate soldiers, identities unknown, circa 1861-1865.

Confederate soldier, identity unknown, circa 1861-1865.

Confederate soldier, identity unknown, circa 1861-1865.

Confederate soldier, identity unknown, circa 1861-1865.

Confederate soldier, identity unknown, circa 1861-1865.

Confederate soldier, identity unknown, circa 1861-1865.

Confederate soldier, identity unknown, circa 1861-1865.

Confederate soldier (left) and civilian (right), identities unknown, circa 1861-1865.

Confederate soldier, identity unknown, circa 1861-1865.

Confederate soldiers, identities unknown, circa 1861-1865.

Confederate soldier, identity unknown, circa 1861-1865.

Confederate soldier, identity unknown, circa 1861-1865.

Confederate soldier, identity unknown, circa 1861-1865.

Confederate soldier, identity unknown, circa 1861-1865.

Confederate soldier, identity unknown, circa 1861-1865.

Confederate soldier, identity unknown, circa 1861-1865.

Confederate soldier, identity unknown, circa 1861-1865.

Confederate soldier, identity unknown, circa 1861-1865.

Confederate soldier, identity unknown, circa 1861-1865.

Confederate soldier, identity unknown, circa 1861-1865.

Confederate soldier, identity unknown, circa 1861-1865.

Confederate soldier, identity unknown, circa 1861-1865.

Confederate soldier, identity unknown, circa 1861-1865.

Confederate soldier, identity unknown, circa 1861-1865.

Confederate soldier, identity unknown, circa 1861-1865.

Confederate soldier, identity unknown, circa 1861-1865.

Confederate soldier, identity unknown, circa 1861-1865.

Confederate soldier, identity unknown, circa 1861-1865.

Confederate soldier, identity unknown, circa 1861-1865.

Confederate soldier, identity unknown, circa 1861-1865.

Confederate soldier, identity unknown, circa 1861-1865.

Confederate soldier, identity unknown, circa 1861-1865.

Confederate soldier, identity unknown, circa 1861-1865.

Confederate Colonel Alexander R. Chisolm, circa 1861-1865.

Confederate soldier, identity unknown, circa 1861-1865.

Confederate soldier, identity unknown, circa 1861-1865.

Confederate soldier, identity unknown, circa 1861-1865.

Confederate soldier, identity unknown, circa 1861-1865.

Confederate soldier, identity unknown, circa 1861-1865.

Confederate soldier, identity unknown, circa 1861-1865.

Confederate soldier, identity unknown, circa 1861-1865.

Confederate soldier, identity unknown, circa 1861-1865.

Confederate soldier, identity unknown, circa 1861-1865.

Confederate soldier, identity unknown, circa 1861-1865.

Confederate soldier, identity unknown, circa 1861-1865.

Confederate soldier, identity unknown, circa 1861-1865.

Confederate soldier, identity unknown, circa 1861-1865.

Confederate soldier, identity unknown, circa 1861-1865.

Confederate soldier, identity unknown, circa 1861-1865.

Confederate soldier, identity unknown, circa 1861-1865.

Confederate soldier, identity unknown, circa 1861-1865.

Confederate soldier, identity unknown, circa 1861-1865.

Confederate soldier, identity unknown, circa 1861-1865.

Confederate soldier, identity unknown, circa 1861-1865.

Confederate soldier, identity unknown, circa 1861-1865.

Confederate soldier, identity unknown, circa 1861-1865.

Confederate soldier, identity unknown, circa 1861-1865.

Confederate soldier, identity unknown, circa 1861-1865.

Confederate soldier, identity unknown, circa 1861-1865.

Confederate soldier, identity unknown, circa 1861-1865.

Confederate soldier, identity unknown, circa 1861-1865.

Confederate soldier, identity unknown, circa 1861-1865.

Confederate soldier, identity unknown, circa 1861-1865.

Confederate soldier, identity unknown, circa 1861-1865.

Confederate soldier, identity unknown, circa 1861-1865.

Confederate soldier, identity unknown, circa 1861-1865.

Confederate soldier, identity unknown, circa 1861-1865.

Confederate soldier, identity unknown, circa 1861-1865.

Confederate soldier, identity unknown, circa 1861-1865.

Confederate soldier, identity unknown, circa 1861-1865.

Confederate soldier, identity unknown, circa 1861-1865.

Confederate soldier, identity unknown, circa 1861-1865.

Confederate soldier, identity unknown, circa 1861-1865.

Confederate soldier, identity unknown, circa 1861-1865.

Confederate soldier, identity unknown, circa 1861-1865.

Confederate soldier, identity unknown, circa 1861-1865.

Confederate soldier, identity unknown, circa 1861-1865.

Confederate soldier, identity unknown, circa 1861-1865.

Confederate soldiers, identities unknown, circa 1861-1865.

Confederate soldier, identity unknown, circa 1861-1865.

Confederate soldier, identity unknown, circa 1861-1865.

Confederate soldier, identity unknown, circa 1861-1865.

Confederate soldier, identity unknown, circa 1861-1865.

Confederate soldier, identity unknown, circa 1861-1865.

Confederate woman holding photo of a Confederate soldier, identities unknown, circa 1861-1865.

Confederate soldier, identity unknown, circa 1861-1865.

Confederate boy holding photo of a Confederate soldier, identities unknown, circa 1861-1865.

Confederate family, identities unknown, circa 1861-1865.

Confederate soldier, identity unknown, circa 1861-1865.

Confederate soldier, identity unknown, circa 1861-1865.

Confederate soldier, identity unknown, circa 1861-1865.

Confederate soldier, identity unknown, circa 1861-1865.

Confederate soldier, identity unknown, circa 1861-1865.

Confederate soldier, identity unknown, circa 1861-1865.

Confederate soldier, identity unknown, circa 1861-1865.

Confederate soldier, identity unknown, circa 1861-1865.

Confederate soldier and his wife, identities unknown, circa 1861-1865.

Confederate soldier, identity unknown, circa 1861-1865.

Confederate soldier, identity unknown, circa 1861-1865.

Confederate soldier and his wife, identities unknown, circa 1861-1865.

Confederate soldier, identity unknown, circa 1861-1865.

Confederate soldier, identity unknown, circa 1861-1865.

Confederate soldier, identity unknown, circa 1861-1865.

Confederate soldier, identity unknown, circa 1861-1865.

Confederate soldier, identity unknown, circa 1861-1865.

Confederate soldier, identity unknown, circa 1861-1865.

Confederate soldier, identity unknown, circa 1861-1865.

Confederate soldier, identity unknown, circa 1861-1865.

Confederate soldier, identity unknown, circa 1861-1865.

Confederate soldier, identity unknown, circa 1861-1865.

Confederate soldier, identity unknown, circa 1861-1865.

Confederate soldier, identity unknown, circa 1861-1865.

Wife of Confederate soldier to the upper left, identity unknown, circa 1861-1865.

Confederate girl, identity unknown, perhaps related to the couple above, circa 1861-1865.

Confederate boy, identity unknown, perhaps related to the couple above, circa 1861-1865.

Confederate soldier, identity unknown, circa 1861-1865.

Confederate soldier, identity unknown, circa 1861-1865.

Confederate soldiers, identities unknown, circa 1861-1865.

Confederate soldier, identity unknown, circa 1861-1865.

Confederate soldier, identity unknown, circa 1861-1865.

Confederate soldier, identity unknown, circa 1861-1865.

Confederate soldier, identity unknown, circa 1861-1865.

Confederate soldier, identity unknown, circa 1861-1865.

Confederate soldier, identity unknown, circa 1861-1865.

Confederate soldier, identity unknown, circa 1861-1865.

Confederate soldier, identity unknown, circa 1861-1865.

Confederate soldier, identity unknown, circa 1861-1865.

Confederate soldier, identity unknown, circa 1861-1865.

Confederate soldier, identity unknown, circa 1861-1865.

Confederate soldier, identity unknown, circa 1861-1865.

Confederate soldier, identity unknown, circa 1861-1865.

Confederate soldier, identity unknown, circa 1861-1865.

Confederate soldier, identity unknown, circa 1861-1865.

Confederate soldier, identity unknown, circa 1861-1865.

Confederate soldier, identity unknown, circa 1861-1865.

Confederate soldier, identity unknown, circa 1861-1865.

Confederate soldiers, identities unknown, circa 1861-1865.

Confederate soldiers, identities unknown, circa 1861-1865.

Confederate Private Ed Landvoigt (left) of the 1st Confederate Cavalry Regiment, and two unidentified soldiers, circa 1862-1865.

Confederate soldier, identity unknown, circa 1861-1865.

Confederate Lieutenant Daniel Giraud Wright, circa 1861-1865.

Confederate Private David Lowry, circa 1861-1865.

Confederate soldier, identity unknown, circa 1861-1865.

Confederate Private Walter K. Thompson, circa 1862-1865.

Confederate soldiers, identities unknown, circa 1861-1865.

Brothers: Confederate Private William Savage Moore and Confederate Private John C. Moore, circa 1861-1865.

Confederate Private Thaddeus W. Clary, circa 1861-1865.

Confederate Second-Sergeant John Hamilton Ervine, circa 1861-1865.

Confederate soldier, identity unknown, circa 1861-1865.

Confederate soldier, identity unknown, circa 1861-1865.

Confederate Lieutenant-Colonel Legh Wilbur Reid, circa 1864-1865.

Confederate Lieutenant-Colonel Harry W. Gilmor, 1862.

Confederate Sergeant Joseph Kennedy Marshall (far left) with unidentified Confederate prisoners, Union prison, Rock Island, Illinois, 1863.

Confederate soldier, identity unknown, circa 1861-1865.

Confederate soldier, identity unknown, circa 1861-1865.

Confederate soldier, first name unknown, surname Long, circa 1861-1865.

Confederate captain, first name unknown, surname Andrew, circa 1861-1865.

Confederate soldier, identity unknown, circa 1861-1865.

Confederate soldier, identity unknown, circa 1861-1865.

Confederate soldier, identity unknown, circa 1861-1865.

Confederate soldier, identity unknown, circa 1861-1865.

Confederate soldier, identity unknown, circa 1861-1865.

Confederate soldier, William Jenkins, circa 1861-1865.

Confederate soldier, identity unknown, circa 1861-1865.

Confederate soldier, identity unknown, circa 1861-1865.

Confederate soldiers, identities unknown, circa 1861-1865.

Confederate soldier, identity unknown, circa 1861-1865.

Confederate soldiers, identities unknown, circa 1861-1865.

Confederate soldier, identity unknown, circa 1861-1865.

Confederate soldiers, identities unknown, circa 1861-1865.

Confederate Private Charles Chapman (left), other Confederate soldier (right) unknown, circa 1861-1865.

Confederate soldier, identity unknown, circa 1861-1865.

Confederate soldier, identity unknown, circa 1861-1865.

Confederate soldier, identity unknown, circa 1861-1865.

Confederate soldier, identity unknown, circa 1861-1865.

Confederate soldier and woman, identities unknown, 1862.

Confederate Dr. Edmund Lewis Massie, circa 1861-1865.

Confederate soldier, identity unknown, circa 1861-1865.

Confederate Private R. Cecil Johnson, 1862.

Confederate soldier J. Ray, circa 1861-1865.

Confederate Sergeant B. F. Smith, circa 1861-1865.

Confederate Captain William Pratt Parks, circa 1862-1863.

Confederate Private Archibald Magill Smith, circa 1861-1865.

Confederate Private Henry Hobson, circa 1862-1865.

Confederate Captain Joel Houghton Abbott, circa 1861-1865.

Confederate soldier John B. Williamson, circa 1861-1865.

Confederate soldier Jesse Woodson James, 1864.

Confederate soldier Frank James, circa 1898.

Confederate Colonel John Singleton Mosby, circa 1861-1865.

Confederate Private Ezekiel Chandler, 1862.

Confederate Captain Henry Fitzgerald, with his wife Catherine and their son Alexander H. Fitzgerald, circa 1863-1864.

Confederate Sergeant Patrick L. Henry, circa 1861-1865.

Confederate First-Lieutenant James N. Bell with his wife Emmeline and their daughter Nannie Claudia Bell, circa 1861-1865.

Brothers: Confederate First-Lieutenant Daniel J. Hatter and Confederate soldier Thomas A. Hatter, circa 1861-1865.

Confederate Lieutenant George Washington, circa 1863-1

Confederate Private John Poole Sellman, probably circa 1861-1865.

Confederate surgeon Dr. Henry Brisco, circa 1862-1865.

Confederate Colonel Henry Marshall Ashby, circa 1861-1865.

Confederate Major Bernard Likens Wolff, circa 1861-1865.

Confederate Captain Levi Harrison Cullers, circa 1861-1865.

Confederate Private Andrew J. Stokes, circa 1862-1865.

Confederate Captain James Thomas Bussey, circa 1863.

Confederate Captain Wilson M. Cary Jr., circa 1861-1865.

Confederate Captain James Corbin Blackford, circa 1861-1864.

Confederate Private Reggie T. Wingfield and Confederate Private Hamden T. Flay, circa 1861-1865.

Confederate soldier, identity unknown, circa 1861-1865.

Confederate Private Stephen Pollard, circa 1861-1865.

Confederate Lieutenant E. S. Hull, circa 1861-1865.

Confederate soldier Thomas Isaiah Booker, circa 1861-1863.

Confederate Colonel Osmun Latrobe, circa 1861-1865.

Confederate officer, identity unknown, circa 1861-1865.

Confederate Private John De Pe, circa 1861-1865.

Confederate Lieutenant John Summerfield Lanier, circa 1861-1863.

Confederate Captain Frederick Morgan Colston, circa 1861-1865.

Confederate Major Elliott Johnston, circa 1861-1863.

Confederate officer, identity unknown, circa 1861-1865.

Confederate officer, identity unknown, circa 1861-1865.

Confederate officer, identity unknown, circa 1861-1865.

Confederate officer, identity unknown, circa 1861-1865.

Confederate prisoners at their barracks, Camp Douglas Prison, Chicago, Illinois, circa 1862-1865.

Confederate soldier, identity unknown, circa 1861-1865.

Confederate soldier, identity unknown, circa 1861-1865.

Confederate Captain James Dugan Gist, circa 1861-1863.

Confederate officer, identity unknown, circa 1861-1865.

Brothers: Confederate soldiers James McHenry Howard and David Ridgely Howard, circa 1864-1870.

Confederate soldier Peter Jones, circa 1861-1865.

Confederate soldier, surname Bowman, circa 1861-1865.

Confederate Private William B. Todd, circa 1863-1865.

Confederate Sergeant Andrew Martin Chandler (left) and Confederate soldier Silas Chandler (right), circa 1861-1863.

Confederate Dr. Alexander Harris and his wife, circa 1870.

Confederate Lieutenant Horatio J. David, circa 1861-1865.

Confederate Private W. T. Harbison, circa 1861-1865.

Confederate Sergeant William T. Belew, circa 1861-1865.

Confederate Private Samuel H. Wilhelm, circa 1862-1863.

Confederate Captain William W. Cosby, circa 1861-1865.

Confederate Private Tom Lumpkin, circa 1861-1865.

Confederate soldier William Snodgrass, circa 1861-1865.

Confederate Private Luther Hart Clapp, circa 1861-1862.

Confederate Private David M. Thatcher, circa 1861-1865.

Confederate Captain George Riggs Gaither, circa 1861-1863.

Confederate Private Peter Lauck Kurtz, circa 1861-1865.

Confederate Corporal L. Purnell, circa 1861-1865.

Confederate officer Jesse Sharpe Barnes, circa 1861-early 1862.

"White and black slaves from New Orleans" (original title by New York photographer.) Isaac White (left), Augusta Broujey (right), and unidentified emancipated woman (center), possibly Mary Johnson, 1863.

Confederate spy Rose O'Neal Greenhow, circa 1855-1865.

Confederate spy Belle Boyd, circa 1860-1865.

Confederate Third-Lieutenant John Alphonso Beall, circa 1861-1865.

Confederate Captain Daniel Turrentine, circa 1861-1865.

Confederate Private William H. Presgraves, circa 1861-1865.

Confederate Private Albert B. Martin, circa 1861-1865.

Confederate Captain James H. M. Neblett, 1862.

Confederate Private Simeon J. Crews, circa 1861-1865.

Confederate Private Alexander T. Harris, 1862.

Confederate Private Joseph T. Rowland, circa 1861-1862.

Confederate Captain William H. Powell, circa 1862-1865.

Confederate Major Charles Jones Green, circa 1861-1865.

Confederate Major Robert Olin Peatross, circa 1861-1865.

Confederate Colonel Felix L. Price, circa 1861-1862.

Confederate Major John C. Pelham, circa 1861-1863.

Confederate Private George H. Williamson, circa 1861-1864.

Confederate soldier Oney Swepson A. Brock, circa 1862.

Confederate soldier John W. Anthony, 1862.

Confederate Private David C. Colbert, circa 1861-1865.

Confederate Private William Anthony Holland, circa 1861-1865.

Confederate soldier Theophilus Mann, circa 1864-1865.

Brothers: Confederate Private Stephen D. Boynton (left) and Confederate Private Moses M. Boynton (right), circa 1861-1862.

Confederate soldier Joshua Whitten, circa 1861-1865.

Confederate Colonel Joseph Walker, circa 1861-1865.

Confederate Lieutenant Parish (first name unknown), 1863.

Confederate soldier Achilles Perrin, 1861.

Brother and sister: Confederate Private Edward A. Cary and Emma J. Cary, circa 1861-1862.

Confederate Captain David Thompson, circa 1861-1865.

Confederate Lieutenant William Sharpe Barnes, circa 1861-1865.

Confederate soldier Lewis Hicks, 1863.

Confederate Private Eli Franklin, circa 1861-1865.

Confederate Sergeant William T. Biedler, circa 1861-1865.

Confederate Captain William A. Hill, 1865.

Confederate Major Thomas B. Beall, circa 1861-1865.

Confederate Private Peter S. Arthur, 1861.

Confederate Captain George W. Hackworth, circa 1861-1865.

Confederate Private Parris P. Casey, circa 1861-1863.

Confederate Lieutenant William Bowen Gallaher, 1861.

Confederate Lieutenant Hiram L. Hendley, circa 1861-1865.

Confederate Captain Alexander Dixon Payne, circa 1861-1865.

Confederate Private Thomas McCreary, circa 1861-1865.

Confederate Private James B. McCutchan, circa 1861-1865.

Confederate Private Amos Guise, circa 1862-1865.

Confederate Private Peter H. Bird, circa 1861-1862.

Confederate Private Richard F. Bernard, circa 1861-1864.

Confederate Private Samuel T. Cowley, circa 1861-1864.

Confederate Private Reuben Goodson, circa 1862-1864.

Confederate Private Silas A. Shirley, circa 1861-1864.

Confederate Private Henry Augustus Moore, circa 1861-1863.

Confederate Sergeant John E. Barlow, circa 1861-1865.

Confederate Private Lucien Love, circa 1863-1864.

Confederate Private Archibald D. Council, circa 1861-1863.

Confederate Private John P. Alldredge, 1862.

Confederate Corporal John Wesley Edmunds, circa 1861-1863.

Confederate Sergeant Elijah McClanahan Ingles, circa 1861-1865.

Brothers: Confederate Private Thomas D. Hilliard and Confederate Corporal John Hilliard, circa 1862-1864.

Confederate Private James W. McCulloch, 1862.

Confederate Private Stanford Lea Jesse, circa 1861-1862.

Confederate Private Benjamin W. Varnell, circa 1862-1865.

Confederate Private Elijah S. Leach, circa 1862-1865.

Confederate Lieutenant Smith Whitfield, circa 1861-1865.

Confederate Private Charles H. Ruff, circa 1861-1865.

Confederate Private William Baxter Ott, 1861.

Confederate Private J. P. Robertson, 1861.

Confederate Lieutenant Thomas S. McLane, circa 1862-1864.

Confederate Private George Hamilton Guinn, circa 1861-1865.

Confederate Lieutenant Robert Pryor James, circa 1861-1865.

Confederate Lieutenant Colonel Warren Adams, circa 1861-1865.

Confederate Private William H. Austin, circa 1861-1865.

Confederate Private Thomas P. Devereux, 1864.

Confederate Lieutenant John T. Fraley, circa 1861-1864.

Confederate soldier James W. Millner, circa 1861-1865.

Confederate soldier W. P. Ward, 1863.

Confederate Private John G. Lee, circa 1861-1865.

Confederate Private Jackson A. Davis, circa 1861-1865.

Confederate Private William Stone, circa 1862-1865.

Confederate Lieutenant Andrew J. Gahagan, circa 1862-1865.

Confederate Captain William F. McRorie, circa 1861-1864.

Confederate woman, identity unknown, circa 1864-1865.

Confederate Private John James Audubon Powell and Confederate Private Van Franklin Garrett, circa 1864-1865.

Confederate Corporal James Adril Wisenbaker and his wife Sarah A. Dasher Wisenbaker, circa 1861-1865.

Confederate Sergeant Robert Taylor Knox, circa 1861-1865.

Confederate First-Lieutenant Thomas S. Nelson, circa 1861-1864.

Confederate Private Christopher Swann, 1862-1865.

Confederate Trooper Robert Vaughan, circa 1861-1865.

Confederate Lieutenant-Colonel Alexander Swift Pendleton, circa 1861-1864.

Confederate Second-Lieutenant Theodore S. Garnett, circa 1863-1865.

Confederate Chaplain Robert Bean Sutton, circa 1861.

Confederate Private W. R. Clack, circa 1861-1865.

Confederate Private Philip A. Nail, circa 1861-1862.

Confederate Private John J. Rhodes, circa 1863-1865.

Confederate Private William Henry, circa 1863.

Confederate Private Charles L. Poteat, circa 1862-1865.

Confederate Colonel Jarrett Norfleet Harrell, circa 1861-1863.

Confederate Corporal C. Dorma Clarke, circa 1863.

Confederate Corporal Edward Lindsey Clarke, circa 1861-1865.

Confederate Corporal Adrian D. Price, circa 1860-1862.

Confederate Sergeant John R. A. Reece, 1861-1862.

Confederate Private Joseph Lorenzo Bilisoly, 1864.

Confederate Chaplain Richard McIlwaine with his cousin Frances S. McIlwaine (standing left), and her two daughters Mary and Sarah, circa 1861-1862.

Confederate Private John Rigby, circa 1861-1865.

Brothers: Confederate Corporal Abel Hoyle Gantt (left) and Confederate Private Marcus A. Gantt (right), circa 1861-1862.

Confederate Colonel Lawrence Massillon Keitt, circa 1862-1864.

Confederate First-Lieutenant Daniel Bowly Thompson with his fiancée Achsah Carroll Winn, circa 1863.

Confederate Colonel Montfort Sydney Stokes, circa 1861-1862.

Confederate Captain Eugene A. Hawkins, Confederate Colonel William H. Willis, and Confederate Captain Howard Tinsley, circa 1861-1864.

Confederate Captain Samuel S. Biddle, circa 1862-1865.

Confederate Major Philip Van Horn Weems, circa 1862-1864.

Confederate Private Robert M. Wilson, circa 1862-1865.

Confederate Captain John Louis Smith, circa 1861-1864.

Confederate Private S. B. Ray, circa 1861-1862.

Confederate Captain Henry Zollicoffer Wellmore, circa 1861.

Confederate Colonel William W. Ward, circa 1864.

Confederate Captain Robert Emmet Robinson, circa 1860.

Confederate Private George Addison Cooke, circa 1861-1864.

Confederate Private John Cocke Ashton, circa 1864-1865.

Confederate Private Addison J. Bowman, circa 1861-1862.

Confederate Sergeant James Bishop White, circa 1861-1865.

Confederate Corporal John Agee Booker, circa 1861-1862.

Confederate First-Lieutenant Job Dillingham Barnard, circa 1861-1865.

Confederate Captain William Clarke Quantrill, circa 1861-1865.

Confederate engineer David Bullock Harris, circa 1863.

Confederate Private Thomas F. Bates, circa 1861-1865.

Confederate Private C. C. Wenner, circa 1861-1865.

Confederate Corporal Bernard Bluecher Graves, circa 1863.

Confederate Private Enoch Hooper Cook Jr., circa 1861-1865.

Confederate Private Thomas Kitchen, circa 1861-1865.

Confederate Private James S. Dodd, circa 1861-1865.

Confederate Private John Lawrence Rapier, circa 1861-1865.

Confederate veteran John P. Funk, circa 1920.

Confederate Private Thomas Bobo, circa 1861-1865.

Confederate veteran James Monroe Fears (right) with his son, World War I soldier Arch Franklin Fears (left), circa 1917.

Confederate admiral Franklin Buchanan, circa 1861-1865.

Confederate naval officer, identity unknown, circa 1861-1865.

Confederate naval Commander William F. Lynch, circa 1861-1865.

Confederate Lieutenant Morris Greenwall, circa 1861-1865.

The End

Female Confederate prisoner, identity unknown, circa 1861-1865.

APPENDIX A
CONFEDERATE CHAIN OF COMMAND
From Highest Rank to Lowest Rank
1861-1865

President (Commander-in-Chief)
General-in-Chief
General
Lieutenant-General
Major-General
Brigadier-General
Colonel
Lieutenant-Colonel
Major
Captain
First-Lieutenant
Second-Lieutenant
Sergeant-Major
Quartermaster-Sergeant
Ordnance-Sergeant
First-Sergeant
Sergeant
Corporal
Private
Musician

(NOTE: The Confederate ranking structure differs according to various sources.)

Illustration from the Confederate government's 1861 publication: *Uniform and Dress of the Confederate States.*

APPENDIX B

Information on the
JEFFERSON DAVIS CABINET

Top Officials of
The Confederate States of America

Jefferson Davis: President
Alexander Hamilton Stephens: Vice-President

1. Robert Augustus Toombs: Secretary of State.
2. Robert Mercer Taliaferro Hunter: Secretary of State.
3. William Montague Browne: Secretary of State.
4. Christopher Gustav Memminger: Secretary of the Treasury.
5. George Alfred Trenholm: Secretary of the Treasury.
6. Leroy Pope Walker: Secretary of War.
7. George Wythe Randolph: Secretary of War.
8. Gustavus Woodson Smith: Secretary of War.
9. James Alexander Seddon: Secretary of War.
10. John Cabell Breckinridge: Secretary of War.
11. Stephen Russell Mallory: Secretary of the Navy.
12. Henry Thomas Ellett: Postmaster General.
13. John Henninger Reagan: Postmaster General.
14. Judah Philip Benjamin: Secretary of State, Attorney General, Secretary of War.
15. Thomas Bragg: Attorney General.
16. Thomas Hill Watts: Attorney General.
17. George Davis: Attorney General.
18. Wade Rutledge Keyes: Attorney General.

Vice-President Stephens (sitting left center) and President Davis (sitting right center), surrounded by the administration's six cabinet members; Montgomery, Alabama, 1861.

Davis personally appointed his first cabinet members. Of this early process he later remarked:

> "Unencumbered by any other consideration than the public welfare, having no friends to reward or enemies to punish, it resulted that not one of those who formed my first cabinet had borne to me the relation of close personal friendship or had political claims on me; indeed, with two of them I had no personal acquaintance."[1]

Davis' cabinet was comprised of six positions:

1. Secretary of State.
2. Secretary of the Navy.
3. Attorney General.
4. Postmaster General.
5. Secretary of the Treasury.
6. Secretary of War.

As noted on the previous page, over time 18 different men occupied the cabinet, the high number due to the constantly shifting priorities and events brought on by Lincoln's sudden and unconstitutional invasion of the South.

Several individuals declined the invitation to join Davis' cabinet for various reasons, while some cabinet members later resigned their position to join the C.S. military as war loomed over the new republic.[2]

In all, four different individuals served as secretary of state, two as secretary of the treasury, six as secretary of war, two as postmaster general, and five as attorney general. Judah P. Benjamin, the "brains of the Confederacy," served in three different cabinet positions. Only one cabinet position retained its original member from 1861-1865: secretary of the navy.[3]

---

1. *Confederate Veteran*, January 1908, Vol. 16, No. 1, p. 48.
2. For more on Jefferson Davis see my book, *The Quotable Jefferson Davis: Selections From the Writings and Speeches of the Confederacy's First President*. Franklin, TN: Sea Raven Press, 2011.
3. For more on Alexander H. Stephens see my books: 1) *The Alexander H. Stephens Reader: Excerpts From the Works of a Confederate Founding Father*. Spring Hill, TN: Sea Raven Press, 2013; 2) *The Quotable Alexander H. Stephens: Selections From the Writings and Speeches of the Confederacy's First Vice President*. Spring Hill, TN: Sea Raven Press, 2013 Sesquicentennial Civil War Edition.

APPENDIX C

Supplemental List of the Presumed 474

GENERAL OFFICERS
OF THE REGULAR CONFEDERATE STATES ARMY

By Rank - Compiled By Southerners

MY LIST OF 430 GENERALS MERGED WITH *CONFEDERATE VETERANS'* LIST OF 474 GENERALS.

NOTES: a) Asterisks indicate the 52 men from *Confederate Veteran's* list of Confederate generals that I did not include in my list of Confederate generals (see my footnote at end of list). b) My comments are in brackets.

KEY: Name, State, Date of Rank

- 8 FULL GENERALS -
Listed chronologically by date of rank (includes state)
Samuel Cooper, Virginia, May 1861; adjt. and inspector general.
Albert S. Johnston, Texas, May 1861.
Robert E. Lee, Virginia, June 1861.
Joseph E. Johnston, Virginia, July 1861.
Pierre G. T. Beauregard, Louisiana, July 1861.
Braxton Bragg, Louisiana, April 1862.
E. Kirby-Smith, Florida, February 1864; general in Provisional Army, C.S.A.
John B. Hood, Tex., July 1864; general with temporary rank.

- 19 LIEUTENANT GENERALS -
Listed chronologically by date of rank (includes state)
Simon B. Buckner, Kentucky, September 1861.
James Longstreet, Alabama, October 1862.
Leonidas Polk, Louisiana, October 1862.
Theophilus H. Holmes, North Carolina, October 1862.
William J. Hardee, Georgia, October 1862.
Thomas J. Jackson, Virginia, October 1862.
John C. Pemberton, Virginia, October 1862.
Richard S. Ewell, Virginia, May 1863.
Ambrose P. Hill, Virginia, May 1863.
Daniel H. Hill, North Carolina, July 1863.
Richard Taylor, Louisiana, April 1864.
Jubal A. Early, Virginia, May 1864.
Richard H. Anderson, South Carolina, May 1864.
Stephen D. Lee, South Carolina, June 1864.
Alex P. Stewart, Tennessee, June 1864.
Wade Hampton, South Carolina, February 1865.
John B. Gordon, Georgia, February 1865.
Joseph Wheeler, Georgia, February 1865.
Nathan B. Forrest, Tennessee, February 1865.

- 82 MAJOR GENERALS -
Listed chronologically by date of rank (includes state)

David E. Twiggs, Georgia, May 1861.
Earl Van Dorn, Mississippi, September 1861.
Gustavus W. Smith, Kentucky, September 1861.
Benjamin Huger, South Carolina, October 1861.
J. Bankhead Magruder, Virginia, October 1861.
Mansfield Lovell, Maryland, October 1861.
George B. Crittenden, Kentucky, November 1861.
William W. Loring, Florida, February 1862.
Sterling Price, Missouri, March 1862.
Benjamin F. Cheatham, Tennessee, March 1862.
Samuel Jones, Virginia, March 1862.
John P. McCown, Tennessee, March 1862.
Jones M. Withers, Alabama, April 1862.
Thomas C. Hindman, Arkansas, April 1862.
John C. Breckenridge, Kentucky, April 1862.
Lafayette McLaws, Georgia, May 1862.
J. E. B. Stuart, Virginia, July 1862.
Samuel G. French, Mississippi, August 1862.
Carter L. Stevenson, Virginia, October 1862.
George E. Pickett, Virginia, October 1862.
David R. Jones, Georgia, October 1862.
John H. Forney, Alabama, October 1862.
Dabney H. Maury, Virginia, November 1862.
Martin L. Smith, Florida, November 1862.
John G. Walker, Missouri, November 1862.
Arnold Elzey, Maryland, December 1862.
Franklin Gardner, Louisiana, December 1862.
Patrick R. Cleburne, Arkansas, December 1862.
Isaac R. Trimble, Maryland, January 1863.
Daniel S. Donelson, Tennessee, January 1863.
W. H. C. Whiting, Mississippi, February 1863.
Edward Johnson, Virginia, February 1863.
Robert E. Rodes, Alabama, May 1863.
W. H. T. Walker, Georgia, May 1863.
Henry Heth, Virginia, May 1863.
John S. Bowen, Missouri, May 1863.
Robert Ransom, Jr., North Carolina, May 1863.
William D. Pender, North Carolina, May 1863.
Cadmus M. Wilcox, Tennessee, August 1863.
Jeremy F. Gilmer, North Carolina, August 1863.
Fitzhugh Lee, Virginia, August 1863.
William Smith, Virginia, August 1863.
Howell Cobb, Georgia, September 1863.
John A. Wharton, Texas, November 1863.
William T. Martin, Mississippi, November 1863.
Charles W. Field, Kentucky, February 1864.
J. Patton Anderson, Florida, February 1864.
William B. Bate, Tennessee, February 1864.
Samuel B. Maxey, Texas, April 1864.
Robert F. Hoke, North Carolina, April 1864.
W. H. F. Lee, Virginia, April 1864.
James L. Kemper, Virginia, March 1864.
Jolin S. Marmaduke, Missouri, March 1864.
Camille J. Polignac, France, April 1864.
James F. Fagan, Arkansas, April 1864.
James B. Gordon, North Carolina, May 1864.

Joseph B. Kershaw, South Carolina, May 1864.
Bushrod R. Johnson, Tennessee, May 1864.
Stephen D. Ramseur, North Carolina, June 1864.
Edward C. Walthall, Mississippi, June 1864.
Henry D. Clayton, Alabama, July 1864.
William Mahone, Virginia, July 1864.
John C. Brown, Tennessee, August 1864.
Lunsford L. Lomax, Virginia, August 1864.
Matthew C. Butler, South Carolina, September 1864.
Henry W. Allen, Louisiana, 1864.
John Pegram, Virginia, 1864.
Ambrose R. Wright, Georgia, November 1864.
Pierce M. B. Young, Georgia, December 1864.
Thomas L. Rosser, Texas, November 1864.
G. W. C. Lee, Virginia, January 1865.
William Preston, Kentucky, January 1865.
William B. Taliaferro, Virginia, January 1865.
Bryan Grimes, North Carolina, February 1865.
William W. Allen, Alabama, March 1865.
W. Y. C. Humes, Tennessee, March 1865.
Matt W. Ransom, North Carolina, 1865.
Thomas J. Churchill, Arkansas, March 1865.
Harry T. Hays, Louisiana, April 1865.
Evander M. Law, Alabama, April 1865.
Martin W. Gary, South Carolina, 1865.
Reuben Davis (my addition, L.S.).

- 365 BRIGADIER GENERALS -
Listed alphabetically by surname, with state and date of rank
*Charles W. Adams, Arkansas, 1862.
Daniel W. Adams, Louisiana, May 1862.
John Adams, Tennessee, December 1862.
*Wirt Adams, Mississippi, September 1863.
E. Porter Alexander, Georgia, February 1864.
George B. Anderson, North Carolina, June 1862.
George T. Anderson, Georgia, November 1862.
Joseph R. Anderson, Virginia, September 1861.
Robert H. Anderson, Georgia, July 1864.
Samuel R. Anderson, Tennessee, July 1861.
James J. Archer, Maryland, June 1862.
L. A. Armistead, Virginia, April 1862.
Frank C. Armstrong, Louisiana, January 1863.
Turner Ashby, Virginia, May 1862.
*Arthur P. Bagly, Texas, 1864.
Alpheus Baker, Alabama, March 1864.
Lawrence S. Baker, North Carolina, July 1863.
William E. Baldwin, Mississippi, September 1862.
William Barksdale, Mississippi, August 1862.
*James W. Barnes, Texas, 1864.
Rufus Barringer, North Carolina, June 1864.
John D. Barry, North Carolina, August 1864.
*William S. Barry, Mississippi, 1862.
Seth M. Barton, Virginia, March 1862.
*Francis S. Bartow, Georgia, July 1861.
Cullen A. Battle, Alabama, August 1863.
*John R. Baylor, Texas, 1864.
Richard L. T. Beale, Virginia, February 1865.
W. N. R. Beall, Arkansas, April 1862.

Barnard E. Bee, South Carolina, June 1861.
Hamilton P. Bee, Texas, March 1862.
Tyree H. Bell, Tennessee, November 1863.
Henry L. Benning, Georgia, January 1863.
Samuel Benton, Mississippi, July 1864.
Albert G. Blanchard, Louisiana, September 1861.
William R. Boggs, Georgia, November 1862.
M. L. Bonham, South Carolina, April 1861.
*Pinckney D. Bowles, Alabama, April 1865.
L. O'B. Branch, North Carolina, November 1861.
William L. Brandon, Mississippi, June 1864.
W. F. Brantley, Mississippi, July 1864.
John Bratton, South Carolina, May 1864.
*Joseph L. Brent, Louisiana, October 1864.
Theodore W. Brevard, Florida, March 1865.
William M. Browne, Georgia, December 1864.
Goode Bryan, Georgia, August 1863.
Abraham Buford, Kentucky, September 1862.
Michael J. Bulger (my addition, L.S.).
Robert Bullock, Florida, November 1864.
William L. Cabell, Virginia, January 1863.
Alex W. Campbell, Tennessee, March 1864.
James Cantey, Alabama, January 1863.
Ellison Capers, South Carolina, November 1864.
William H. Carroll, Tennessee, October 1861.
John C. Carter, Tennessee, July 1864.
James R. Chalmers, Mississippi, February 1862.
John R. Chambliss, Jr., Virginia, December 1863.
James Chestnut, Jr., South Carolina, April 1864.
Robert H. Chilton, Virginia, October 1862.
James H. Clanton, Alabama, November 1863.
Charles Clark, Mississippi, May 1861.
John B. Clark, Jr., Missouri, March 1864.
Thomas L. Clingman, North Carolina, May 1862.
Thomas R. R. Cobb, Georgia, November 1862.
Philip St. George Cocke, Virginia, October 1861.
Francis M. Cockrell, Missouri, July 1863.
Alfred H. Colquitt, Georgia, September 1862.
Raleigh E. Colston, Virginia, December 1861.
James Conner, South ina, June 1864.
Philip Cook, Georgia, August 1864.
John R. Cooke, North Carolina, November 1862.
Douglas H. Cooper, Mississippi, May 1863.
M. D. Corse, Virginia, November 1862.
George B. Cosby, Kentucky, January 1863.
*John Z. Cox, Tennessee, 1865.
William R. Cox, North Carolina, May 1864.
*C. C. Crews, Georgia, 1865.
Alfred Cumming, Georgia, October 1862.
Junius Daniel, North Carolina, September 1862.
Henry B. Davidson, Tennessee, August 1863.
Joseph R. Davis, Mississippi, September 1862.
W. G. M. Davis, Florida, November 1862.
James Dearing, Virginia, 1864.
Zachariah C. Deas, Alabama, December 1862.
*Xavier B. DeBray, Texas, April 1864.
Julius A. DeLagnel [or de Lagnel], Virginia, April 1862.
James Deshler, Georgia, July 1863.

George G. Dibrell, Tennessee, July 1864.
*Archibald J. Dobbins, Arkansas, 1864.
Thomas P. Dockery, Arkansas, August 1863.
George P. Doles, Georgia, November 1862.
Thomas F. Drayton, South Carolina, September 1861.
Dudley M. Du Bose, Georgia, November 1864.
Basil W. Duke, Kentucky, September 1864.
Johnson K. Duncan, Louisiana, January 1862.
John Echols, Virginia, April 1862.
M. D. Ector, Texas, August 1862.
Stephen Elliott, Jr., South Carolina, May 1864.
Clement A. Evans, Georgia, May 1864.
Nathan G. Evans, South Carolina, October 1861.
Thomas T. Fauntleroy (my addition, L.S.).
William S. Featherston, Mississippi, March 1862.
Samuel W. Ferguson, Mississippi, July 1863.
Joseph J. Finegan, Florida, April 1862.
Jesse J. Finley, Florida, November 1863.
*John C. Fiser, Mississippi, 1865.
John B. Floyd, Virginia, May 1861.
William H. Forney, Alabama, November 1864.
John W. Frazer, Alabama, May 1863.
Daniel M. Frost, Missouri, March 1862.
Burkett [Birkett] D. Fry, Alabama, May 1864.
Richard M. Gano, Kentucky, 1865.
*Edward W. Gantt, Arkansas, 1862.
William M. Gardner, Georgia, November 1861.
Samuel Garland, Jr., Virginia, May 1862.
Richard B. Garnett, Virginia, November 1861.
Robert S. Garnett, Virginia, June 1861.
Isham W. Garrott, Alabama, May 1863.
Lucius J. Gartrell, Georgia, August 1864.
Richard C. Gatlin, North Carolina, July 1861.
Samuel J. Gholson, Mississippi, May 1864.
*George C. Gibbs, North Carolina, 1864.
Randall L. Gibson, Louisiana, January 1864.
Victor J. B. Girardey, Georgia, July 1864.
States Rights Gist, South Carolina, March 1862.
Adley H. Gladden, Louisiana, September 1861.
A. C. Godwin, North Carolina, August 1864.
James M. Goggin, Virginia, December 1864.
George W. Gordon, Tennessee, August 1864.
Josiah Gorgas, Alabama, November 1864.
Daniel C. Govan, Arkansas, December 1863.
Archibald Gracie, Jr., Alabama, November 1862.
Hiram B. Granberry, Texas, February 1864.
Henry Gray, Louisiana, March 1865.
John B. Grayson, Louisiana, August 1861.
Martin E. Green, Missouri, July 1862.
Thomas Green, Texas, May 1863.
*Colton Greene, Missouri, 1863.
Elkanah Greer, Texas, October 1862.
John Gregg, Texas, August 1862.
Maxcy Gregg, South Carolina, December 1861.
Richard Griffith, Mississippi, November 1861.
*J. Warren Grigsby, Kentucky, 1864.
James Hagan, Alabama, February 1865 (my addition, L.S.).
Johnson Haygood [Hagood], South Carolina, July 1862.

*Moses W. Hannon, Alabama, 1865.
Roger W. Hanson, Kentucky, December 1862.
William P. Hardeman, Texas, March 1865.
N. H. Harris, Mississippi, January 1864.
*George P. Harrison, Jr., Georgia, February 1865.
James E. Harrison, Texas, December 1864.
*Richard Harrison, Texas, 1865.
Thomas Harrison, Texas, January 1865.
Robert Hatton, Tennessee, May 1862.
James M. Hawes, Kentucky, March 1862.
Alex T. Hawthorne, Arkansas, February 1864.
Louis Hebert, Louisiana, May 1862.
Paul O. Hebert, Louisiana, August 1861.
Ben Hardin Helm, Kentucky, March 1862.
*Robert J. Henderson, Georgia, 1864.
Edward Higgins, Louisiana, October 1863.
Benjamin J. Hill, Tennessee, October 1864.
George B. Hodge, Kentucky, November 1863.
Joseph S. [L.] Hogg, Texas, February 1862.
*William J. Hoke, North Carolina, 1865.
James T. Holtzclaw, Alabama, July 1864.
Benjamin G. Humphreys, Mississippi, August 1863.
Eppa Hunton, Virginia, August 1863.
John D. Imboden, Virginia, January 1863.
Alfred Iverson, Jr., Georgia, November 1862.
*Sidney D. Jackman, Missouri, February 1865.
Henry R. Jackson, Georgia, June 1861.
John K. Jackson, Georgia, January 1862.
William H. Jackson, Tennessee, December 1862.
William L. Jackson, Virginia, September 1864.
Albert G. Jenkins, Virginia, August 1862.
Micah Jenkins, South Carolina, July 1862.
Adam R. Johnson, Texas, August 1864.
Bradley T. Johnson, Maryland, June 1864.
George D. Johnston, Alabama, July 1864.
Robert D. Johnston, North Carolina, September 1863.
*A. C. Jones, Tennessee, 1865.
John M. Jones, Virginia, May 1863.
John R. Jones, Virginia, June 1862.
William E. Jones, Virginia, September 1862.
Thomas Jordan, Virginia, April 1862.
James [John] H. Kelly, Alabama, November 1863.
John D. Kennedy, South Carolina, December 1864.
*William H. King, Georgia, April 1864.
William W. Kirkland, North Carolina, August 1863.
James H. Lane, North Carolina, November 1862.
Walter P. Lane, Texas, March 1865.
Alex R. Lawton, Georgia, April 1861.
Danville Leadbetter, Alabama, February 1862.
Edwin G. Lee, Virginia, September 1864.
Collette Leventhorpe, North Carolina, February 1865.
Joseph H. Lewis, Kentucky, September 1863.
*L. M. Lewis, Missouri, November 1864.
William G. Lewis, North Carolina, May 1864.
St. John R. Liddell, Louisiana, July 1862.
Robert D. Lilley, Virginia, May 1864.
*Henry Little, Missouri, April 1862.
Thomas M. Logan, South Carolina, February 1865.

Armistead L. Long, Virginia, September 1863.
Mark P. Lowrey, Mississippi, October 1863.
Robert Lowry, Mississippi, February 1865.
Hylan B. Lyon, Kentucky, June 1864.
*Hinchie P. Mabry, Texas, March 1862.
William W. Mackall, Maryland, February 1862.
*Robert P. MacLay, Arkansas, 1865.
William MacRae, North Carolina, June 1864.
James P. Major, Missouri, July 1863.
George Maney, Tennessee, April 1862.
Arthur M. Manigault, South Carolina, April 1863.
Humphrey Marshall, Kentucky, October 1861.
*John Marshall, Texas, 1865.
James G. Martin, North Carolina, May 1862.
*John D. Martin, Mississippi, 1865.
John McCausland, Virginia, May 1864.
William McComb, Tennessee, January 1865.
*Thomas H. McCray, Arkansas, 1863.
Benjamin McCulloch, Texas, May 1861.
Henry E. McCulloch, Texas, March 1862.
Samuel McGowan, South Carolina, January 1863.
James M. McIntosh, Florida, January 1862.
James A. McMurray, Tennessee.
Evander McNair, Arkansas, November 1862.
Dandridge McRae, Arkansas, November 1862.
Hugh W. Mercer, Georgia, October 1861.
*William R. Miles, Louisiana, 1864.
William Miller, Florida, August 1864.
Young M. Moody, Alabama, March 1865.
John C. Moore, Texas, May 1862.
Patrick T. Moore, Virginia, May 1864.
*S. P. Moore, South Carolina, 1865.
John H. Morgan, Kentucky, December 1862.
John T. Morgan, Alabama, November 1863.
*Alfred Mouton, Louisiana, April 1862.
*Thomas T. Munford, Virginia, November 1864.
Allison Nelson, Texas, September 1862.
Francis T. Nicholls, Louisiana, October 1862.
Edward A. O'Neal, Alabama, June 1863.
Richard L. Page, Virginia, March 1864.
Joseph B. Palmer, Tennessee, November 1864.
Mosby M. Parsons, Missouri, November 1862.
Elisha F. Paxton, Virginia, November 1862.
William H. Payne, Virginia, November 1864.
William R. Peck, Louisiana, February 1865.
William N. Pendleton, Virginia, March 1862.
Abner Perrin, South Carolina, September 1863.
Edward A. Perry, Florida, August 1862.
William F. Perry, Alabama, February 1865.
James J. Pettigrew, North Carolina, February 1862.
Edmund W. Pettus, Alabama, September 1863.
*Charles W. Phifer, Arkansas, 1862.
Albert Pike, Arkansas, August 1861.
Gideon J. Pillow, Tennessee, July 1861.
Lucius E. Polk, Arkansas, December 1862.
Carnot Posey, Mississippi, November 1862.
John S. Preston, South Carolina, June 1864.
Roger A. Pryor, Virginia, April 1862.

William A. Quarles, Tennessee, August 1863.
Gabriel J. Rains, North Carolina, September 1861.
*George W. Rains, Georgia, 1865.
James E. Rains, Tennessee, November 1862.
*Horace Randal, Texas, April 1864.
George W. Randolph, Virginia, February 1862.
*John C. Reid, Alabama, 1864.
Alex W. Reynolds, Virginia, September 1863.
*Arthur E. Reynolds, Mississippi, March 1865.
Daniel H. Reynolds, Arkansas, March 1864.
Robert V. Richardson, Tennessee, December 1863.
Roswell S. Ripley, South Carolina, August 1861.
J. Selden Roane, Arkansas, March 1862.
William P. Roberts, North Carolina, February 1865.
Beverley H. Robertson, Virginia, June 1862.
Felix H. Robertson, Texas, July 1864.
Jerome B. Robertson, Texas, November 1862.
Philip D. Roddey, Alabama, August 1863.
Lawrence S. Ross, Texas, December 1863.
*Reuben R. Ross, Texas, 1865.
Edmund W. Rucker, 1865 (my addition, L.S.).
Daniel Ruggles, Virginia, August 1861.
*W. W. Russell, Alabama, 1864.
Albert Rust, Arkansas, March 1862.
John C. C. Sanders, Alabama, May 1864.
Alfred M. Scales, North Carolina, June 1863.
Thomas M. Scott, Louisiana, May 1864.
William R. Scurry, Texas, September 1862.
Claudius W. Sears, Mississippi, March 1864.
Paul J. Semmes, Georgia, March 1862.
Jacob H. Sharp, Mississippi, July 1864.
Joseph O. Shelby, Missouri, December 1863.
Charles M. Shelley, Alabama, September 1864.
*William P. Shindler, South Carolina, 1865.
Francis A. Shoup, Florida, September 1862.
Henry H. Sibley, Louisiana, June 1861.
James P. Simms, Georgia, November 1864.
W. Y. Slack, Missouri, April 1862.
James E. Slaughter, Virginia, March 1862.
James A. Smith, Tennessee, September 1863.
Preston Smith, Tennessee, October 1862.
Thomas B. Smith, Tennessee, July 1864.
William D. Smith, Georgia, July 1862.
*John L. T. Sneed, Tennessee, May 1861.
G. Moxley Sorrel, Georgia, October 1864.
Leroy A. Stafford, Louisiana, October 1863.
Peter B. Starke, Mississippi, November 1864.
William E. Starke, Louisiana, August 1862.
William Steele, Texas, September 1862.
*A. E. Steen, Missouri, April 1862.
George H. Steuart, Maryland, March 1862.
Clement H. Stevens, South Carolina, January 1864.
Walter H. Stevens, Virginia, August 1864.
Isaac M. St. John, Georgia, February 1865.
Marcellus A. Stovall, Georgia, January 1863.
Otho F. Strahl, Tennessee, July 1863.
James C. Tappan, Arkansas, November 1862.
Thomas H. Taylor, Kentucky, November 1862.

James B. Terrill, Virginia, May 1864.
William Terry, Virginia, May 1864.
William R. Terry, Virginia, May 1864.
Allen Thomas, Louisiana, February 1864.
Bryan M. Thomas, Louisiana, August 1864.
Edward L. Thomas, Georgia, November 1862.
*M. Jeff Thompson, Missouri, 1861.
Lloyd Tilghman, Kentucky, October 1861.
Robert Toombs, Georgia, July 1861.
Thomas F. Toon, North Carolina, May 1864.
Edward D. Tracy, Georgia, August 1862.
James H. Trapier, South Carolina, October 1861.
William F. Tucker, Mississippi, March 1864.
Robert C. Tyler, Tennessee, February 1864.
Robert B. Vance, North Carolina, March 1863.
Alfred J. Vaughan, Tennessee, November 1863.
John C. Vaughn, Tennessee, September 1862.
John B. Villepigue, South Carolina, March 1862.
*William B. Wade, North Carolina, January 1863.
Henry H. Walker, Virginia, July 1863.
James A. Walker, Virginia, May 1863.
Leroy P. Walker, Alabama, September 1861.
Lucius M. Walker, Tennessee, March 1862.
*R. Lindsay Walker, Virginia, February 1865.
William S. Walker, Florida, October 1862.
Richard Waterhouse, Jr., Texas, March 1865.
Stand Watie, Indian Territory, May 1864.
Thomas N. Waul, Texas, September 1863.
David A. Weisiger, Virginia, May 1864.
Gabriel C. Wharton, Virginia, July 1863.
John W. Whitfield, Texas, May 1863.
William [Williams] C. Wickham, Virginia, September 1863.
Louis T. Wigfall, Texas, October 1861.
John S. Williams, Kentucky, April 1862.
*Edward Willis, Georgia, 1864.
Claudius C. Wilson, Georgia, November 1863.
Charles S. Winder, Maryland, March 1862.
John H. Winder, Maryland, June 1861.
Henry A. Wise, Virginia, June 1861.
William T. Wofford, Georgia, January 1863.
Sterling A. M. Wood, Alabama, January 1862.
*Gilbert J. Wright, Georgia, 1864.
Marcus J. Wright, Tennessee, December 1862.
Zebulon York, Louisiana, May 1864.
William H. Young, Texas, August 1864.
Felix K. Zollicoffer, Tennessee, July 1861.[4]

---

4. This list combines my own personal generals list with the list of generals from *Confederate Veteran* (see the January 1908 issue, Vol. 16, No. 1, pp. 45-48). While *Confederate Veteran* perhaps overgenerously finds that there were 474 generals, my own research yields a much more conservative total number of 430. Other modern historians have determined that there were even less than 430. It must be kept in mind that *legal* generalship in the C.S.A. typically required 1) *nomination* by a general, followed by, 2) *appointment* by President Davis, and finally, 3) *confirmation* by the Confederate senate. Some 52 of the men *Confederate Veteran* recognized as generals in 1908 were never submitted to this customary process—which is why I have not included them in my list. In any event, due to both inaccurate records and loss of records, as well as ongoing debates over *official* and *legitimate* nominations, assignments, commissions, promotions, appointments, confirmations, and dates, it is doubtful that any two lists will ever agree.

Confederate veterans: Private John J. McLendon, Thomas W. Morrison, Private Cornelius C. Bowman, Private Thomas J. Watkins, Private William A. Smith, Private Edmund F. Fenton, and Colonel Risden T. Bennett, circa 1910.

BIBLIOGRAPHY

And Suggested Reading

Note: My pro-South readers are to be advised that the majority of the books listed here are anti-South in nature (some extremely so), and were written primarily by Liberal elitist, socialist, communist, and Marxist authors who loathe the South, and typically the United States and the U.S. Constitution as well. Despite this, as a scholar I find these titles indispensable, for *an honest evaluation of Lincoln's War is not possible without studying both the Southern and the Northern versions*—an attitude, unfortunately, completely lacking among pro-North historians (who read and study only their own ahistorical version). Still, it must be said that the material contained in these absurd and often mean-spirited works is largely the result of a century and a half of Yankee myth, falsehoods, cherry-picking, slander, redaction, sophistry, editorializing, anti-South propaganda, outright lies, and junk research, as modern pro-North writers merely copy one another's errors without ever looking at the original 19th-Century sources. This type of literature, filled as it is with both misinformation and disinformation, is called "scholarly" and "objective" by pro-North advocates. In the process, the mistakes and lies in these fact-free, fault-ridden, South-shaming, historically inaccurate works have been magnified over the years, and the North's version of the "Civil War" has come to be accepted as the only legitimate one. Indeed, it is now the only one known by most people. That over 95 percent of the titles in most of my bibliographies fall into the anti-South category is simply a reflection of the enormous power and influence that the sociopolitical Left—our nation's cultural ruling class—has long held over America's education system, libraries, publishing houses, and media (paper and electronic). My books serve as a small rampart against the overwhelming tide of radical Leftists, anti-South fascists, Liberals, cultural Marxists, and political elites, all who are working hard to obliterate Southern culture and guarantee that you will never learn the Truth about Lincoln and his War on the Constitution and the American people.

Alexander, Edward Porter. *Military Memoirs of a Confederate.* New York: Charles Scribner's Sons, 1907.
American Biography: A New Cyclopedia. New York: The American Historical Society, 1918.
Andrews, Elisha Benjamin. *History of the United States: From the Earliest Discovery of America to the Present Time.* 5 vols. 1894. New York: Charles Scribner's Sons, 1925 ed.
Armstrong, J. M. *The Biographical Encyclopedia of Kentucky of the Dead and Living Men of the Nineteenth Century.* Cincinnati, OH: J. M. Armstrong and Co., 1878.
Ashe, Samuel A'Court. *History of North Carolina.* 2 vols. Greensboro, NC: Charles L. Van Noppen, 1908.
Atkinson, William B. (ed.). *A Biographical Dictionary of Contemporary American Physicians and Surgeons.* Philadelphia, PA: D. G. Brinton, 1880.
Bailey, Thomas A. *The American Spirit: United States History as Seen by Contemporaries.* Boston, MA: D. C. Heath and Co., 1965.
Banta, Theodore Melvin. *Sayre Family: Lineage of Thomas Sayre A Founder of Southampton.* New York: The De Vinne Press, 1901.
Benson, Al, Jr., and Walter Donald Kennedy. *Lincoln's Marxists.* Gretna, LA: Pelican, 2011.
Blay, John S. *The Civil War: A Pictorial Profile.* New York: Thomas Y. Crowell Co., 1958.
Blue and Gray: The Patriotic Magazine, Vol. 2, July-December 1893. Philadelphia, PA: The Patriotic American Co., 1893.
Boatner, Mark Mayo, III. *The Civil War Dictionary.* 1959. New York: David McKay Co., 1988 ed.
Bowman, John S. (ed.). *Encyclopedia of the Civil War.* North Dighton, MA: JG Press, 1992.
Boyd, James P. *Parties, Problems, and Leaders of 1896: An Impartial Presentation of Living National Questions.* Chicago, IL: Publishers' Union, 1896.
Bradford, James C. (ed.). *Atlas of American Military History.* Oxford, UK: Oxford University Press, 2003.
Brewer, Willis. *Alabama: Her History, Resources, War Record, and Public Men; From 1540 to 1872.* Montgomery, AL: self-published, 1872.
Brock, Robert Alonzo (ed.). *Southern Historical Society Papers.* 52 vols. Richmond, VA: Southern Historical Society, 1876-1943.
Browder, Earl. *Lincoln and the Communists.* New York: Workers Library Publishers, Inc., 1936.
Brown, John Howard (ed.). *Lamb's Biographical Dictionary of the United States.* Boston, MA: James H. Lamb Co., 1900.

Bryan, William Jennings. *The First Battle: A Story of the Campaign of 1896*. Chicago, IL: W. B. Conkey Co., 1896.
Buchanan, Lamont. *A Pictorial History of the Confederacy*. New York: Crown Publishers, 1951.
Buford, Marcus Bainbridge. *A Genealogy of the Buford Family in America*. San Francisco, CA: self-published, 1903.
Burns, James MacGregor. *The Vineyard of Liberty*. New York: Alfred A. Knopf, 1982.
Capers, Walter B. *The Soldier-Bishop, Ellison Capers*. New York: Neale Publishing Co., 1912.
Chesnut, Mary Boykin. *A Diary From Dixie*. (Isabella D. Martin and Myrta Lockett Avary, eds.) London, UK: D. Appleton and Co., 1905.
Christian, George Llewellyn. *Abraham Lincoln: An Address Delivered Before R. E. Lee Camp, No. 1 Confederate Veterans at Richmond, VA, October 29, 1909*. Richmond, VA: L. H. Jenkins, 1909.
———. *A Capitol Disaster: A Chapter of Reconstruction in Virginia*. Richmond, VA: self-published, 1915.
———. *Confederate Memories and Experiences*. Richmond, VA: self-published, 1915.
Confederate States Government. *Uniform and Dress of the Army of the Confederate States*. Richmond, VA: self-published, 1861.
Confederate Veteran (Sumner Archibald Cunningham, ed.). 40 vols. Nashville, TN: Confederate Veteran, 1893-1932.
Connor, Robert D. W. *History of North Carolina*. Chicago, IL: Lewis Publishing Co., 1905.
Cox, William R. *Address on the Life and Character of Maj. Gen. Stephen D. Ramseur*. Raleigh, NC: self-published, 1891.
Cruikshank, George M. *A History of Birmingham and Its Environs: A Narrative Account of Their Historical Progress, Their People, and Their Principle Interests*. Chicago, IL: Lewis Publishing Co., 1920.
Current, Richard N. (ed.). *The Confederacy*. New York: Macmillan, 1993.
Cyclopedia of Eminent and Representative Men of the Carolinas of the Nineteenth Century. Madison, WI: Brant and Fuller, 1892.
Davis, Jefferson. *The Rise and Fall of the Confederate Government*. 2 vols. New York: D. Appleton and Co., 1881.
Davis, Varina. *Jefferson Davis, Ex-President of the Confederate States of America: A Memoir by His Wife*. 2 vols. New York: Belford Co., 1890.
Davis, William C. *Look Away! A History of the Confederate States of America*. New York: The Free Press, 2002.
De Bolt, Mary M. *Lineage Book: National Society of the Daughters of the American Revolution*. Washington, D.C.: Judd and Detweiler, 1925.
DeLand, T. A., and A. Davis Smith (eds.). *Northern Alabama: Historical and Biographical*. Birmingham, AL: self-published, 1888.
Denison, Frederic. *Shot and Shell: The Third Rhode Island Heavy Artillery Regiment in the Rebellion, 1861-1865*. Providence, RI: J. A. Reid and R. A. Reid, 1879.
Dodd, Bella. *School of Darkness*. New York: P. J. Kennedy and Sons, 1954.
Donald, David (ed.). *Divided We Fought: A Pictorial History of the War, 1861-1865*. New York: Macmillan Co., 1961 ed.
Dorsey, Sarah Anne. *Recollections of Henry Watkins Allen, Brigadier-General Confederate States Army, Ex-Governor of Louisiana*. New York: M. Doolady, 1866.
Drake, Francis S. *Dictionary of American Biography*. Boston, MA: Houghton, Osgood and Co., 1879.
DuBose, John Witherspoon. *The Life and Times of William Lowndes Yancey*. Birmingham, AL: Roberts and Son, 1892.
———. *General Joseph Wheeler and the Army of Tennessee*. New York: Neale Publishing Co., 1912.
Duke, Basil Wilson. *Reminiscences of General Basil W. Duke, C.S.A.* New York: Doubleday, Page and Co., 1911.
Duval, Mary V. *History of Mississippi and Civil Government*. Louisville, KY: self-published, 1892.
Eicher, John H., and David J. Eicher. *Civil War High Commands*. Stanford, CA: Stanford University Press, 2001.
Eliot, Ellsworth. *West Point in the Confederacy*. New York: G. A. Baker and Co., 1941.
Encyclopedia Britannica: A Dictionary of Arts, Sciences, and General Literature (ninth ed.). New York: Henry G. Allen Co., 1890.
Evans, Clement Anselm (ed.). *Confederate Military History*. 12 vols. Atlanta, GA: Confederate Publishing Co., 1899.
Evans, Lawton Bryan. *A History of Georgia for Use in Schools*. New York: American Book

Company, 1908.
Everett, Lloyd Tilghman. *Living Confederate Principles: A Heritage For All Time*. Ballston, VA: Yexid Publishing Co., 1921.
Fleming, Walter F., et al. (eds.). *The South in the Building of the Nation*. 12 vols. Richmond, VA: Southern Publication Society, 1909.
Forty-Second Annual Reunion of the Association Graduates of the United States Military Academy, at West Point, New York. Saginaw, MI: self-published, 1911.
Franklin, John Hope. *Reconstruction After the Civil War*. Chicago, IL: University of Chicago Press, 1961.
Freeman, Douglas Southall. *A Calendar of Confederate Papers, With a Bibliography of Some Confederate Publications*. Richmond, VA: The Confederate Museum, 1908.
French, Samuel Gibbs. *Two Wars: An Autobiography of Gen. Samuel G. French, An Officer in the Armies of the United States and the Confederate States, a Graduate from the U.S. Military Academy, West Point, 1843*. Nashville, TN: Confederate Veteran, 1901.
Fullerton, Dan C. *Armies in Gray: The Organizational History of the Confederate States Army in the Civil War*. Baton Rouge, LA: Louisiana State University Press, 2017.
Furnas, J. C. *The Americans: A Social History of the United States, 1587-1914*. New York: G. P. Putnam's Sons, 1969.
Garner, Charles K. *A Dictionary of All Officers, Who Have Been Commissioned, or Have Been Appointed and Served, in the Army of the United States, Since the Inauguration of Their First President, in 1789, to the First January 1853*. New York: D. Van Nostrand, 1860.
Gordon, John Brown. *Reminiscences of the Civil War*. New York: Charles Scribner's Sons, 1903.
Grissom, Michael Andrew. *Southern by the Grace of God*. 1988. Gretna, LA: Pelican, 1995 ed.
Grun, Bernard. *The Timetables of History: A Horizontal Linkage of People and Events*. 1946. New York: Touchstone, 1982 ed.
Hagood, Johnson. *Memoirs of the War of Secession: From the Original Manuscripts of Johnson Hagood, Brigadier-General, C.S.A*. Columbia, SC: The State Co., 1910.
Hale, Will T., and Dixon L. Merritt. *A History of Tennessee and Tennesseans: The Leaders and Representative Men in Commerce, Industry and Modern Activities*. Chicago, IL: Lewis Publishing Co., 1913.
Hall, Granville Davisson. *Lee's Invasion of Northwest Virginia in 1861*. Chicago, IL: Mayer and Miller Co., 1911.
Hamilton, J. G. de Roulhac (ed.). *The Papers of Thomas Ruffin*. Raleigh, NC: North Carolina Historical Commission, 1920.
Hancock, Richard R. *Hancock's Diary: Or, A History of the Second Tennessee Confederate Cavalry, With Sketches of First and Seventh Battalions; Also, Portraits and Biographical Sketches*. 2 vols. in 1. Nashville, TN: self-published, 1877.
Hart, Albert Bushnell (ed.). *American History Told by Contemporaries*. 4 vols. New York: Macmillan Co., 1901.
Hasselberg, P. D. (ed.). *Parliamentary Debates: First Session, Fortieth Parliament, 1982, House of Representatives* (Vol. 445). Wellington, New Zealand: Government Printer, 1982.
Hempstead, Fay. *A Pictorial History of Arkansas: From Earliest Times to the Year 1890*. St. Louis, MO: N. D. Thompson, 1890.
Henry, Robert Selph. *The Story of the Confederacy*. 1931. New York: Konecky and Konecky, 1999 ed.
Hesseltine, William B. *Confederate Leaders in the New South*. Baton Rouge, LA: Louisiana State University Press, 1950.
Hole, Charles. *A Brief Biographical Dictionary*. New York: Hurd and Houghton, 1866.
Hood, John Bell. *Advance and Retreat: Personal Experiences in the United States and Confederate Armies*. Philadelphia, PA: Press of Burk and M'Fetridge, 1880.
Hotchkiss, Jedediah, and William Allan. *The Battle-Fields of Virginia: Chancellorsville; Embracing the Operations of the Army of Northern Virginia, From the First Battle of Fredericksburg to the Death of Lieutenant-General Jackson*. New York: D. Van Nostrand, 1867.
Johnson, Adam Rankin. *The Partisan Rangers of the Confederate States Army*. Louisville, KY: George G. Fetter Co., 1904.
Johnson, Robert Underwood, and Clarence Clough Buel (eds.). *Battles and Leaders of the Civil War*. 4 vols. New York: The Century Co., 1884-1888.
Johnson, Rossiter. *Campfire and Battlefield: An Illustrated History of the Campaigns and Conflicts of the Great Civil War*. New York: Bryan, Taylor and Co., 1894.
——. (ed.) *The Twentieth Century Biographical Dictionary of Notable Americans*. Boston, MA: The Biographical Society, 1904.

Johnston, David Emmons. *A History of Middle New River Settlements and Contiguous Territory.* Huntington, WV: Standard Printing and Publishing Co., 1906.
Johnstone, Huger William. *Truth of War Conspiracy, 1861.* Idylwild, GA: H. W. Johnstone, 1921.
Jones, Charles Colcock. *Georgians During the War Between the States: An Address Delivered Before the Confederate Survivors' Association in Augusta, Georgia, April 26, 1889.* Augusta, GA: Chronicle Publishing Co., 1889.
Jones, Charles Edgeworth. *Georgia in the War, 1861-1865.* Augusta, GA: self-published, 1909.
Jones, John William (ed.). *Southern Historical Society Papers.* 52 vols. Richmond, VA: Southern Historical Society, 1876-1959.
———. *The Davis Memorial Volume; Or Our Dead President, Jefferson Davis and the World's Tribute to His Memory.* Richmond, VA: B. F. Johnson, 1889.
Katcher, Philip. *The Civil War Source Book.* 1992. New York: Facts on File, 1995 ed.
Kellogg, J., J. M. Lucy, J. H. Berry, V. Y. Cook, Charles Coffin, Dan W. Jones. *Confederate Women of Arkansas in the Civil War, 1861-'65: Memorial Reminiscences.* Little Rock, AR: United Confederate Veterans, 1907.
Knight, Lucian Lamar (ed.). *Library of Southern Literature.* New Orleans, LA: Martin and Hoyt Co., 1907.
La Bree, Benjamin (ed.). *The Illustrated Confederate War Journal.* (Monthly periodical). New York: War Journal Publishing Co., 1895.
Lamb, Mrs. Martha J. (ed.). *Magazine of American History, With Notes and Queries* (Vol. 14, July-December 1885). New York: Historical Publication Co., 1885.
Lenin, Vladimir. *"Left Wing" Communism: An Infantile Disorder.* Detroit, MI: The Marxian Educational Society, 1921.
LeVert, Suzanne. *The Civil War Society's Encyclopedia of the Civil War.* New York: Wings Books, 1997.
Little, John Buckner. *History of Butler County, Alabama 1815-1885.* Greenville, AL: self-published, 1885.
Livermore, Thomas L. *Numbers and Losses in the Civil War in America, 1861-65.* 1900. Carlisle, PA: John Kallmann, 1996 ed.
Long, Armistead Lindsay, and Marcus Joseph Wright (eds.). *Memoirs of Robert E. Lee: His Military and Personal History Embracing A Large Amount of Information Hitherto Unpublished.* New York: J. M. Stoddart and Co., 1886.
Long, E. B., and Barbara Long. *The Civil War Day by Day: An Almanac 1861-1865.* Cambridge, MA: Da Capo, 1971.
Longstreet, James. *From Manassas to Appomattox: Memories of the Civil War in America.* Philadelphia, PA: J. B. Lippincott and Co., 1896.
Magliocca, Gerard N. *The Tragedy of William Jennings Bryan: Constitutional Law and the Politics of Backlash.* New Haven, CT: Yale University Press, 2011.
Marx, Karl, and Frederick Engels. *Manifesto of the Communist Party.* Chicago, IL: Charles H. Kerr and Co., 1906.
Maury, Dabney Herndon. *Recollections of a Virginian in the Mexican, Indian, and Civil Wars.* New York: Charles Scribner's Sons, 1894.
McCarty, Burke (ed.). *Little Sermons in Socialism by Abraham Lincoln.* Chicago, IL: The Chicago Daily Socialist, 1910.
McPherson, Edward. *The Political History of the United States of America, During the Great Rebellion.* Washington, D.C.: Philp and Solomons, 1865.
McPherson, James M. *Abraham Lincoln and the Second American Revolution.* New York: Oxford University Press, 1991.
Memorial and Biographical History of North Carolina. Chicago, IL: Lewis Publishing Co., 1891.
Meriwether, Colyer (ed.). *Publications of the Southern History Association.* Washington, D.C.: The Association, 1904.
Meriwether, Elizabeth Avery (pseudonym, "George Edmonds"). *Facts and Falsehoods Concerning the War on the South, 1861-1865.* Memphis, TN: A. R. Taylor and Co., 1904.
Mickle, William English. *Well Known Confederate Veterans and Their War Records.* New Orleans, LA: self-published, 1915.
Miller, Francis Trevelyan, and Robert S. Lanier (eds.). *The Photographic History of the Civil War.* 10 vols. New York: The Review of Reviews Co., 1911.
Minutes of the Eighth Annual Meeting and Reunion of the United Confederate Veterans, Atlanta, GA, July 20-23, 1898. New Orleans, LA: United Confederate Veterans, 1907.
Minutes of the Ninth Annual Meeting and Reunion of the United Confederate Veterans, Charleston, SC,

May 10-13, 1899. New Orleans, LA: United Confederate Veterans, 1907.
Minutes of the Twelfth Annual Meeting and Reunion of the United Confederate Veterans, Dallas, TX, April 22-25, 1902. New Orleans, LA: United Confederate Veterans, 1907.
Moore, Frank (ed.). *The Rebellion Record: A Diary of American Events, With Documents, Narratives, Illustrative Incidents, Poetry, etc.* New York: G. P. Putnam, 1862.
Mosby, John Singleton. *The Memoirs of Colonel John S. Mosby*. Boston, MA: Little, Brown, and Co., 1917.
Muzzey, David Saville. *The United States of America: Vol. 1, To the Civil War*. Boston, MA: Ginn and Co., 1922.
———. *The American Adventure: Vol. 2, From the Civil War*. 1924. New York: Harper and Brothers, 1927 ed.
Neilson, William (ed.). *Webster's Biographical Dictionary*. Springfield, MA: G. and C. Merriam Co., 1943.
Nelke, David I. (ed.). *The Columbian Biographical Dictionary and Portrait Gallery of the Representative Men of the United States*. Chicago, IL: Lewis Publishing Co., 1895.
New Biographical Dictionary. Philadelphia, PA: David McKay, 1893.
Nicolay, John G., and John Hay (eds.). *Abraham Lincoln: A History*. 10 vols. New York: The Century Co., 1890.
———. *Complete Works of Abraham Lincoln*. 12 vols. 1894. New York: Francis D. Tandy Co., 1905 ed.
——— *Abraham Lincoln: Complete Works*. 12 vols. 1894. New York: The Century Co., 1907 ed.
North Carolina University Magazine (Vol. 1, No. 3, 1891). Chapel Hill, NC: Students of the University, 1891.
ORA (full title: *The War of the Rebellion: A Compilation of the Official Records of the Union and Confederate Armies*). 70 vols. Washington, DC: Government Printing Office, 1880.
ORN (full title: *Official Records of the Union and Confederate Navies in the War of the Rebellion*). 30 vols. Washington, DC: Government Printing Office, 1894.
Owen, Thomas McAdory (ed.). *Transactions of the Alabama Historical Society, 1897-1898*. Tuscaloosa, AL: Alabama Historical Society, 1898.
Parry, Melanie (ed.). *Chambers Biographical Dictionary*. 1897. Edinburgh, Scotland: Chambers Harrap, 1997 ed.
Pickett, LaSalle Corbell. *Pickett and His Men*. Philadelphia, PA: J. B. Lippincott Co., 1913.
Pollard, Edward Alfred. *Echos From the South: Comprising the Most Important Speeches, Proclamations, and Public Acts Emanating From the South During the Late War*. New York: E. B. Treat and Co., 1866.
———. *The Lost Cause*. New York: E. B. Treat and Co., 1867.
Rhodes, James Ford. *History of the United States From the Compromise of 1850*. New York: Harper and Brothers, 1900.
Richardson, John Anderson. *Richardson's Defense of the South*. Atlanta, GA: A. B. Caldwell, 1914.
Ridpath, John Clark. *The New Complete History of the United States of America*. Cincinnati, OH: Jones Brothers Publishing Co., 1912.
Rogers, William P. *The Three Secession Movements in the United States: Samuel J. Tilden, the Democratic Candidate for Presidency; the Advisor, Aider and Abettor of the Great Secession Movement of 1860; and One of the Authors of the Infamous Resolution of 1864; His Claims as a Statesman and Reformer Considered*. Boston, MA: John Wilson and Son, 1876.
Rove, Karl. *The Triumph of William McKinley: Why the Election of 1896 Still Matters*. New York: Simon and Schuster, 2015.
Rowland, Dunbar. *Encyclopedia of Mississippi History*. 2 vols. Madison, WI: Selwyn A. Brant, 1907.
Rutherford, Mildred Lewis. *Truths of History: A Fair, Unbiased, Impartial, Unprejudiced and Conscientious Study of History*. Athens, GA: n.p., 1920.
Salley, A. S., Jr. (ed.). *South Carolina Troops in Confederate Service*. Columbia, SC: R. L. Bryan Co., 1913.
Scharf, John Thomas. *History of the Confederate States Navy*. New York: Rogers and Sherwood, 1887.
Seabrook, Lochlainn. *Carnton Plantation Ghost Stories: True Tales of the Unexplained from Tennessee's Most Haunted Civil War House!* 2005. Franklin, TN, 2016 ed.
———. *Nathan Bedford Forrest: Southern Hero, American Patriot*. 2007. Franklin, TN, 2010 ed.
———. *Abraham Lincoln: The Southern View*. 2007. Franklin, TN: Sea Raven Press, 2013 ed.
———. *The McGavocks of Carnton Plantation: A Southern History - Celebrating One of Dixie's Most Noble*

———. *Confederate Families and Their Tennessee Home.* 2008. Franklin, TN, 2011 ed.
———. *A Rebel Born: A Defense of Nathan Bedford Forrest.* 2010. Franklin, TN: Sea Raven Press, 2011 ed.
———. *A Rebel Born: The Screenplay* (for the film). 2011. Franklin, TN: Sea Raven Press.
———. *Everything You Were Taught About the Civil War is Wrong, Ask a Southerner!* 2010. Franklin, TN: Sea Raven Press, revised 2019 ed.
———. *The Quotable Jefferson Davis: Selections From the Writings and Speeches of the Confederacy's First President.* Franklin, TN: Sea Raven Press, 2011.
———. *The Quotable Robert E. Lee: Selections From the Writings and Speeches of the South's Most Beloved Civil War General.* Franklin, TN: Sea Raven Press, 2011 Sesquicentennial Civil War Edition.
———. *Lincolnology: The Real Abraham Lincoln Revealed In His Own Words.* Franklin, TN: Sea Raven Press, 2011.
———. *The Unquotable Abraham Lincoln: The President's Quotes They Don't Want You To Know!* Franklin, TN: Sea Raven Press, 2011.
———. *Honest Jeff and Dishonest Abe: A Southern Children's Guide to the Civil War.* Franklin, TN: Sea Raven Press, 2012.
———. *Encyclopedia of the Battle of Franklin - A Comprehensive Guide to the Conflict that Changed the Civil War.* Franklin, TN: Sea Raven Press, 2012.
———. *The Quotable Nathan Bedford Forrest: Selections From the Writings and Speeches of the Confederacy's Most Brilliant Cavalryman.* Spring Hill, TN: Sea Raven Press, 2012.
———. *Forrest! 99 Reasons to Love Nathan Bedford Forrest.* Spring Hill, TN: Sea Raven Press, 2012.
———. *Give 'Em Hell Boys! The Complete Military Correspondence of Nathan Bedford Forrest.* Spring Hill, TN: Sea Raven Press, 2012.
———. *The Constitution of the Confederate States of America Explained: A Clause-by-Clause Study of the South's Magna Carta.* Spring Hill, TN: Sea Raven Press, 2012 Sesquicentennial Civil War Edition.
———. *The Great Impersonator: 99 Reasons to Dislike Abraham Lincoln.* Spring Hill, TN: Sea Raven Press, 2012.
———. *The Old Rebel: Robert E. Lee As He Was Seen By His Contemporaries.* Spring Hill, TN: Sea Raven Press, 2012 Sesquicentennial Civil War Edition.
———. *The Quotable Stonewall Jackson: Selections From the Writings and Speeches of the South's Most Famous General.* Spring Hill, TN: Sea Raven Press, 2012 Sesquicentennial Civil War Edition.
———. *Saddle, Sword, and Gun: A Biography of Nathan Bedford Forrest for Teens.* Spring Hill, TN: Sea Raven Press, 2013.
———. *The Alexander H. Stephens Reader: Excerpts From the Works of a Confederate Founding Father.* Spring Hill, TN: Sea Raven Press, 2013.
———. *The Quotable Alexander H. Stephens: Selections From the Writings and Speeches of the Confederacy's First Vice President.* Spring Hill, TN: Sea Raven Press, 2013 Sesquicentennial Civil War Edition.
———. *Give This Book to a Yankee! A Southern Guide to the Civil War for Northerners.* Spring Hill, TN: Sea Raven Press, 2014.
———. *The Articles of Confederation Explained: A Clause-by-Clause Study of America's First Constitution.* Spring Hill, TN: Sea Raven Press, 2014.
———. *Confederate Blood and Treasure: An Interview With Lochlainn Seabrook.* Spring Hill, TN: Sea Raven Press, 2015.
———. *Nathan Bedford Forrest and the Battle of Fort Pillow: Yankee Myth, Confederate Fact.* Spring Hill, TN: Sea Raven Press, 2015.
———. *Everything You Were Taught About American Slavery War is Wrong, Ask a Southerner!* Spring Hill, TN: Sea Raven Press, 2015.
———. *Confederacy 101: Amazing Facts You Never Knew About America's Oldest Political Tradition.* Spring Hill, TN: Sea Raven Press, 2015.
———. *The Great Yankee Coverup: What the North Doesn't Want You to Know About Lincoln's War!* Spring Hill, TN: Sea Raven Press, 2015.
———. *Slavery 101: Amazing Facts You Never Knew About America's "Peculiar Institution."* Spring Hill, TN: Sea Raven Press, 2015.
———. *Confederate Flag Facts: What Every American Should Know About Dixie's Southern Cross.* Spring Hill, TN: Sea Raven Press, 2016.
———. *Nathan Bedford Forrest and the Ku Klux Klan: Yankee Myth, Confederate Fact.* Spring Hill, TN: Sea Raven Press, 2016.

———. *Seabrook's Bible Dictionary of Traditional and Mystical Christian Doctrines*. Spring Hill, TN: Sea Raven Press, 2016.
———. *Everything You Were Taught About African-Americans and the Civil War is Wrong, Ask a Southerner!* Spring Hill, TN: Sea Raven Press, 2016.
———. *Nathan Bedford Forrest and African-Americans: Yankee Myth, Confederate Fact*. Spring Hill, TN: Sea Raven Press, 2016.
———. *Women in Gray: A Tribute to the Ladies Who Supported the Southern Confederacy*. Spring Hill, TN: Sea Raven Press, 2016.
———. *Lincoln's War: The Real Cause, the Real Winner, the Real Loser*. Spring Hill, TN: Sea Raven Press, 2016.
———. *The Unholy Crusade: Lincoln's Legacy of Destruction in the American South*. Spring Hill, TN: Sea Raven Press, 2017.
———. *Abraham Lincoln Was a Liberal, Jefferson Davis Was a Conservative: The Missing Key to Understanding the American Civil War*. Spring Hill, TN: Sea Raven Press, 2017.
———. *All We Ask is to be Let Alone: The Southern Secession Fact Book*. Spring Hill, TN: Sea Raven Press, 2017.
———. *The Ultimate Civil War Quiz Book: How Much Do You Really Know About America's Most Misunderstood Conflict?* Spring Hill, TN: Sea Raven Press, 2017.
———. *Rise Up and Call Them Blessed: Victorian Tributes to the Confederate Soldier, 1861-1901*. Spring Hill, TN: Sea Raven Press, 2017.
———. *Victorian Confederate Poetry: The Southern Cause in Verse, 1861-1901*. Spring Hill, TN: Sea Raven Press, 2018.
———. *Confederate Monuments: Why Every American Should Honor Confederate Soldiers and Their Memorials*. Spring Hill, TN: Sea Raven Press, 2018.
———. *The God of War: Nathan Bedford Forrest as He Was Seen by His Contemporaries*. Spring Hill, TN: Sea Raven Press, 2018.
———. *The Battle of Spring Hill: Recollections of Confederate and Union Soldiers*. Spring Hill, TN: Sea Raven Press, 2018.
———. *I Rode With Forrest! Confederate Soldiers Who Served With the World's Greatest Cavalry Leader*. Spring Hill, TN: Sea Raven Press, 2018.
———. *The Battle of Nashville: Recollections of Confederate and Union Soldiers*. Spring Hill, TN: Sea Raven Press, 2018.
———. *The Battle of Franklin: Recollections of Confederate and Union Soldiers*. Spring Hill, TN: Sea Raven Press, 2018.
———. (ed.) *A Short History of the Confederate States of America* (Jefferson Davis, Belford Company, NY, 1890). A Sea Raven Press Reprint. Spring Hill, TN: Sea Raven Press, 2020.
———. (ed.) *Prison Life of Jefferson Davis: Embracing Details and Incidents in his Captivity, With Conversations on Topics of Public Interest* (John J. Craven, Sampson, Low, Son, and Marston, London, UK, 1866). A Sea Raven Press Reprint. Spring Hill, TN: Sea Raven Press, 2020.
———. *What the Confederate Flag Means to Me: Americans Speak Out in Defense of Southern Honor, Heritage, and History*. Spring Hill, TN: Sea Raven Press, 2021.
Seitz, Don Carlos. *Braxton Bragg: General of the Confederacy*. Columbia, SC: The State Co., 1924.
Simpson, Lewis P. (ed.). *I'll Take My Stand: The South and the Agrarian Tradition (by Twelve Southerners)*. 1930. Baton Rouge, LA: Louisiana State University Press, 1977 ed.
Snow, William Parker. *Southern Generals, Their Lives and Campaigns*. New York: Charles B. Richardson, 1866.
Sobel, Robert (ed.). *Biographical Directory of the United States Executive Branch, 1774-1989*. Westport, CT: Greenwood Press, 1990.
Sorrel, Gilbert Moxley. *Recollections of a Confederate Staff Officer*. New York: Neale Publishing Co., 1905.
Steel, Samuel Augustus. *The South Was Right*. Columbia, SC: R. L. Bryan Co., 1914.
Stephens, Alexander Hamilton. *Speech of Mr. Stephens, of Georgia, on the War and Taxation*. Washington, D.C.: J & G. Gideon, 1848.
———. *A Constitutional View of the Late War Between the States; Its Causes, Character, Conduct and Results*. 2 vols. Philadelphia, PA: National Publishing, Co., 1870.
———. *Recollections of Alexander H. Stephens: His Diary Kept When a Prisoner at Fort Warren, Boston Harbour, 1865*. New York: Doubleday, Page, and Co., 1910.
Sterling, Ada (ed.). *A Belle in the Fifties: Memoirs of Mrs. Clay of Alabama, Covering Social and Political Life in Washington and the South, 1853-1866*. New York: Doubleday, Page and Co., 1905.
Taylor, Thomas E. *Running the Blockade: A Personal Narrative of Adventures, Risks, and Escapes*

During the American Civil War. London, UK: John Murray, 1896.
Taylor, Walter Herron. *Four Years With General Lee*. New York: D. Appleton and Co., 1878.
The Lost Cause: A Confederate War Record. (Periodical.) Louisville, KY: United Sons of Confederate Veterans, 1901 series.
The National Cyclopedia of American Biography. New York: James T. White and Co., 1900.
The United States Biographical Dictionary and Portrait Gallery of Eminent and Self-made Men. Chicago, IL: American Biographical Publishing Co., 1877.
Thomas, Emory M. *The Confederate Nation: 1861-1865*. New York: Harper and Row, 1979.
Thompson, Holland. *The New South: A Chronicle of Social and Industrial Evolution*. New Haven, CT: Yale University Press, 1920.
Tyler, Lyon Gardiner (ed.). *Encyclopedia of Virginia Biography*. New York: Lewis Historical Publishing Co., 1915.
United States Government. *List of Staff Officers of the Confederate States Army, 1861-1865*. Washington D.C.: U.S. War Department, 1891.
———. *Annual Report of the American Historical Association for the Year 1897*. Washington D.C.: U.S. Government Printing Office, 1898.
———. *Executive and Congressional Directory of the Confederate States, 1861-1865*. Washington, D.C.: U.S. Record and Pension Office, 1899.
———. *Journal of the Congress of the Confederate States of America, 1861-1865*. Washington, D.C.: U.S. Government Printing Office, 1904.
———. *Memorandum Relative to the General Officers Appointed by the President in the Armies of the Confederate States, 1861-1865*. Washington, D.C.: Military Secretary's Office, U.S. War Department, 1905.
———. *Biographical Directory of the American Congress, 1744-1927*. Washington D.C.: U.S. Government Printing Office, 1923.
———. *Register of Officers of the Confederate States Navy 1861-1865*. Washington D.C.: Office of Naval Records, U.S. Government Printing Office, 1931.
———. *Senators of the United States: A Historical Bibliography*. (Jo Anne Quatannens, ed.) Washington D.C.: U.S. Government Printing Office, 1995.
Warner, Ezra J. *Generals in Gray: Lives of the Confederate Commanders*. 1959. Baton Rouge, LA: Louisiana State University Press, 1989 ed.
———. *Generals in Blue: Lives of the Union Commanders*. 1964. Baton Rouge, LA: Louisiana State University Press, 2006 ed.
Watkins, Sam R. *"Co. Aytch," Maury Grays, First Tennessee Regiment; Or a Side Show of the Big Show*. Chattanooga, TN: self-published, 1900.
Welsh, Jack D. *Medical Histories of Confederate Generals*. Kent, OH: Kent State University Press, 1995.
Wilson, Charles Reagan, and William Ferris (eds.). *Encyclopedia of Southern Culture*. New York: Anchor Books, 1989.
Wilson, James Grant, and John Fiske (eds.). *Appleton's Cyclopedia of American Biography*. New York: D. Appleton and Co., 1888.
Wise, Henry Alexander. *Seven Decades of the Union: The Humanities and Materialism, Illustrated by a Memoir of John Tyler, With Reminiscences of Some of his Great Contemporaries*. Philadelphia, PA: J. B. Lippincott and Co., 1872.
Wright, Marcus Joseph. *General Officers of the Confederate Army*. New York: Neale Publishing Co., 1911.
Woods, Thomas E., Jr. *The Politically Incorrect Guide to American History*. Washington, D.C.: Regnery, 2004.
Woodworth, Steven E. *Jefferson Davis and his Generals: The Failure of Confederate Command in the West*. Lawrence, KS: University Press of Kansas, 1990.
Young, Jesse Bowman. *The Battle of Gettysburg: A Comprehensive Narrative*. New York: Harper and Brothers, 1913.

INDEX

- A -

Abbott, Joel H., 240
Adams, Charles W., 299
Adams, Daniel W., 49, 299
Adams, John, 49, 299
Adams, Warren, 273
Adams, William W., 49
Adams, Wirt, 299
Alexander, Edward P., 26, 49, 299
Alldredge, John P., 269
Allen, Henry W., 50, 299
Allen, William W., 50, 299
Anderson, George B., 50, 299
Anderson, George T., 50, 299
Anderson, James P., 51, 298
Anderson, Joseph R., 51, 299
Anderson, Richard H., 51, 297
Anderson, Robert H., 51, 299
Anderson, Samuel R., 52, 299
Andrew, _____, 232
Anthony, John W., 260
Archer, James J., 52, 299
Armistead, Lewis A., 52, 299
Armstrong, Frank C., 52, 299
Arthur, Peter S., 265
Ashby, Henry M., 243, 299
Ashby, Turner, 53
Ashton, John C., 287
Austin, William H., 274

- B -

Bagly, Arthur P., 299
Baker, Alpheus, 53, 299
Baker, Laurence S., 53, 299
Baldwin, William E., 53, 299
Barksdale, William, 54, 299
Barlow, John E., 269
Barnard, Job D., 288
Barnes, James W., 299
Barnes, Jesse S., 255
Barnes, William S., 263
Barringer, Rufus, 31, 54, 299
Barry, John D., 54, 299
Barry, William S., 299
Barton, Seth M., 54, 299
Bartow, Francis S., 299
Bate, William B., 55, 298
Bates, Thomas F., 289
Battle, Cullen A., 55, 299

Baylor, John R., 299
Beale, Richard L. T., 55, 299
Beall, John A., 257
Beall, Thomas B., 265
Beall, William N. R., 55, 299
Beauregard, Pierre G. T., 56, 297
Bee, Barnard E., 56, 300
Bee, Hamilton P., 56, 300
Belew, William T., 253
Bell, Emmeline, 242
Bell, James N., 242
Bell, Nannie C., 242
Bell, Tyree H., 56, 300
Benjamin, Judah P., 45, 295, 296
Benning, Henry L., 57, 300
Benton, Samuel, 57, 300
Bernard, Richard F. 267
Biddle, Samuel S., 285
Biedler, William T., 264
Bilisoly, Joseph L., 281
Bird, Peter H., 267
Blackford, James C., 245
Blanchard, Albert G., 32, 57, 300
Bobo, Thomas, 291
Boggs, William R., 57, 300
Bonham, Milledge L., 58, 300
Booker, John A., 288
Booker, Thomas I., 246
Bowen, John S., 58, 298
Bowles, Pinckney D., 300
Bowman, _____, 251
Bowman, Addison J., 287
Boyd, Belle, 256
Boynton, Moses M., 261
Boynton, Stephen D., 261
Bragg, Braxton, 30, 58, 297
Bragg, Thomas, 45, 295
Branch, Lawrence O., 58, 300
Brandon, William L., 59, 300
Brantley, William F., 59, 300
Bratton, John, 59, 300
Breckinridge, John C., 44, 59, 295, 298
Brent, Joseph L., 300
Brevard, Theodore W., 60, 300
Brisco, Henry, 243
Brock, Oney S. A., 260
Broujey, Augusta, 256
Brown, John C., 60, 299

Browne, William M., 42, 60, 295, 300
Bryan, Goode, 60, 300
Buchanan, Franklin, 291
Buckner, Simon B., 61, 297
Buel, Clarence C., 13
Buford, Abraham, 61, 300
Bulger, Michael J., 61, 300
Bullock, Robert, 61, 300
Bussey, James T., 244
Butler, Matthew C., 31, 62, 299

- C -

Cabell, William L., 62, 300
Campbell, Alexander W., 62, 300
Cantey, James, 62, 300
Capers, Ellison, 63, 300
Carroll, William H., 63, 300
Carter, John C., 63, 300
Cary, Edward A., 263
Cary, Emma J., 263
Cary, Wilson M., Jr., 245
Casey, Parris P., 265
Chalmers, James R., 63, 300
Chambliss, John R., Jr., 64, 300
Chandler, Andrew M., 252
Chandler, Ezekiel, 241
Chandler, Silas, 252
Chapman, Charles, 236
Cheatham, Benjamin F., 64, 298
Chesnut, James, Jr., 64, 300
Chilton, Robert H., 31, 64, 300
Chisholm, Alexander R., 199
Churchill, Thomas J., 65, 299
Clack, W. R., 279
Clanton, James H., 65, 300
Clapp, Luther H., 254
Clark, Charles, 65, 300
Clark, John B., Jr., 65, 300
Clarke, C. Dorma, 280
Clarke, Edward L., 280
Clary, Thaddeus W., 229
Clayton, Henry D., 66, 299
Cleburne, Patrick R., 66, 298
Cleveland, Grover, 26, 27, 28, 29
Clingman, Thomas L., 66, 300
Cobb, Howell, 66, 298
Cobb, Thomas R. R., 67, 300
Cocke, Philip St. George, 23, 67, 300
Cockrell, Francis M., 26, 67, 300
Colbert, David C., 261
Colquitt, Alfred H., 29, 67, 300

Colston, Frederick M., 248
Colston, Raleigh E., 68, 300
Connor, James, 68, 300
Conrad, Thomas N., 161
Cook, Enoch H., Jr., 289
Cook, Philip, 68, 300
Cooke, George A., 287
Cooke, John R., 68, 300
Cooper, Douglas H., 69, 300
Cooper, Samuel, 32, 69, 297
Corse, Montgomery D., 31, 69, 300
Cosby, George B., 69, 300
Cosby, William W., 253
Council, Archibald D., 269
Cowley, Samuel T., 268
Cox, John Z., 300
Cox, William R., 70, 300
Crews, C. C., 300
Crews, Simeon J., 258
Crittenden, George B., 70, 298
Cullers, Levi H., 244
Cumming, Alfred, 70, 300

- D -

Dana, Charles A., 33
Daniel, Junius, 70, 300
David, Horatio J., 252
Davidson, Henry B., 71, 300
Davis, George, 46, 295
Davis, Jackson A., 275
Davis, Jefferson, 11, 12, 14, 22, 25, 33, 41, 295, 296
Davis, Joseph R., 71, 300
Davis, Reuben, 71, 299
Davis, William G. M., 71, 300
Dearing, James, 72, 300
Deas, Zachariah C., 72, 300
DeBray, Xavier B., 300
de Lagnel, Julius A., 72, 302
De Pe, John, 247
Deshler, James, 72, 300
Devereux, Thomas P., 274
Dibrell, George G., 73, 300
Dobbins, Archibald J., 301
Dockery, Thomas P., 73, 301
Dodd, James S., 290
Doles, George P., 23, 73, 301
Donelson, Daniel S., 73, 298
Dorsey, William H. B., 162
Drayton, Thomas F., 74, 301
DuBose, Dudley M., 74, 301
DuBose, John W., 21

Duke, Basil W., 26, 28-29, 74, 301
Duncan, Johnson K., 74, 301
Dunovant, John, 75

- E -
Early, Jubal A., 75, 297
Echols, John, 75, 301
Ector, Matthew D., 75, 301
Edmunds, John W., 270
Ellett, Henry T., 45, 295
Elliott, Stephen, Jr., 76, 301
Elzey, Arnold, 76, 298
Ervine, John H. 229
Evans, Clement A., 76, 301
Evans, Nathan G., 76, 301
Ewell, Richard S., 77, 297

- F -
Fagan, James F., 28, 77, 298
Fauntleroy, Thomas T., 14, 77, 301
Fears, Arch F., 291
Fears, James M., 291
Featherston, Winfield S., 77, 301
Ferguson, Samuel W., 78, 301
Field, Charles W., 78, 298
Finegan, Joseph J., 78, 301
Finley, Jesse J., 78, 301
Fiser, John C., 301
Fitzgerald, Alexander H., 241
Fitzgerald, Catherine, 241
Fitzgerald, Henry, 241
Flay, Hamden T., 245
Floyd, John B., 79, 301
Forney, John H., 79, 298
Forney, William H., 79, 301
Forrest, Nathan B., 14, 15, 23, 24, 25, 30, 79, 297
Fraley, John T., 274
Franklin, Eli, 264
Frazer, John W., 80, 301
French, Samuel G., 25, 32, 80, 298
Frost, Daniel M., 80, 301
Fry, Birkett D., 80, 301
Funk, John P., 290

- G -
Gahagan, Andrew J., 276
Gaither, George R., 255
Gallaher, William B., 266
Gano, Richard M., 81, 301
Gantt, Abel H., 283
Gantt, Edward W., 301
Gantt, Marcus A., 283

Gardner, Franklin, 81, 298
Gardner, William M., 81, 301
Garland, Samuel, Jr., 81, 301
Garnett, Richard B., 35, 82, 301
Garnett, Robert S., 82, 301
Garnett, Theodore S., 278
Garrett, Van F., 276
Garrott, Isham W., 82, 301
Gartrell, Lucius J., 82, 301
Gary, Martin W., 83, 299
Gatlin, Richard C., 83, 301
George III, King, 12
Gholson, Samuel J., 83, 301
Gibbs, George C., 301
Gibson, Randall L., 29, 83, 301
Gilmer, Jeremy F., 84, 298
Gilmor, Harry W., 230
Girardey, Victor J. B., 84, 301
Gist, James D., 250
Gist, States R., 84, 301
Gladden, Adley H., 30, 84, 301
Godwin, Archibald C., 85, 301
Goggin, James M., 85, 301
Goodson, Reuben, 268
Gordon, George W., 85, 301
Gordon, James B., 85, 298
Gordon, John B., 8, 26, 86, 297
Gorgas, Josiah, 25, 86, 301
Govan, Daniel C., 27, 86, 301
Gracie, Archibald, Jr., 86, 301
Granbury, Hiram B., 87, 301
Grant, Ulysses S., 28, 31
Graves, Bernard B., 289
Gray, Henry, 87, 301
Grayson, John B., 87, 301
Green, Charles J., 259
Green, Colton, 301
Green, Martin E., 87, 301
Green, Thomas, 88, 301
Greenhow, Rose O., 256
Greenwall, Morris, 292
Greer, Elkanah B., 88, 301
Gregg, John, 88, 301
Gregg, Maxcy, 88, 301
Griffith, Richard, 89, 301
Grigsby, J. Warren, 301
Grimes, Bryan, 89, 299
Guinn, George H., 273
Guise, Amos, 267

- H -
Hackworth, George W., 265
Hagan, James, 13, 89, 301

Hagood, Johnson, 18, 29, 89, 301
Hampton, Wade, 30, 90, 297
Hannon, Moses, 301
Hanson, Roger W., 90, 302
Harbison, W. T., 253
Hardee, William J., 23, 90, 297
Hardeman, William P., 29, 90, 302
Harding, John, 24
Harding, Selene, 24
Harrell, Jarrett N., 280
Harris, Alexander, 252
Harris, Alexander T., 258
Harris, David B., 288
Harris, Nathaniel H., 29, 91, 302
Harrison, George P., Jr., 302
Harrison, James E., 91, 302
Harrison, Richard, 302
Harrison, Thomas, 30, 91, 302
Hatter, Daniel J., 242
Hatter, Thomas A., 242
Hatton, Robert H., 32, 91, 302
Hawes, James M., 92, 302
Hawkins, Eugene A., 284
Hawthorn, Alexander T., 92, 302
Hays, Harry T., 30, 31, 92, 299
Hébert, Louis, 92, 302
Hébert, Paul O., 93, 302
Helm, Benjamin H., 93, 302
Henderson, Robert J., 302
Hendley, Hiram L., 266
Henry, Patrick L., 242
Henry, William, 279
Heth, Henry, 93, 298
Hicks, Lewis, 264
Higgins, Edward, 93, 302
Hill, Ambrose P., 94, 297
Hill, Benjamin J., 94, 302
Hill, Daniel H., 25, 94, 297
Hill, William A., 264
Hilliard, John, 270
Hilliard, Thomas D., 270
Hindman, Thomas C., Jr., 94, 298
Hobson, Henry, 239
Hodge, George B., 95, 302
Hogg, Joseph L., 95, 302
Hoke, Robert F., 95, 298, 324
Hoke, William J., 302
Holland, William A., 261
Holmes, Theophilus H., 23, 95, 297
Holtzclaw, James T., 96, 302
Hood, John B., 26, 96, 297
Howard, David R., 251
Howard, James M., 251

Huger, Benjamin, 96, 298
Hull, E. S., 246
Humes, William Y. C., 96, 299
Humphreys, Benjamin G., 29, 97, 302
Hunter, Robert M. T., 42, 295
Hunton, Eppa, 30, 97, 302

- I -
Imboden, John D., 97, 302
Ingles, Elijah M., 270
Iverson, Alfred, Jr., 97, 302

- J -
Jackman, Sidney D., 302
Jackson, Alfred E., 23, 98
Jackson, Henry R., 27, 98, 302
Jackson, John K., 98, 302
Jackson, Thomas J. "Stonewall", 23, 30, 98, 297
Jackson, William H., 24, 99, 302
Jackson, William L., 99, 302
James, Frank, 240
James, Jesse W., 240
James, Robert P., 273
Jenkins, Albert G., 99, 302
Jenkins, Micah, 99, 302
Jenkins, William, 233
Jesse, Stanford L., 271
Johnson, Adam R., 26, 100, 302
Johnson, Bradley T., 100, 302
Johnson, Bushrod R., 25, 100, 299
Johnson, Edward, 23, 100, 298
Johnson, Mary, 256
Johnson, R. Cecil, 238
Johnston, Albert S., 101, 297
Johnston, Elliott, 248
Johnston, George D., 24, 101, 302
Johnston, Joseph E., 101, 297
Johnston, Robert D., 101, 302
Jones, A. C., 302
Jones, David R., 102, 298
Jones, John M., 102, 302
Jones, John R., 102, 302
Jones, Peter, 251
Jones, Samuel, 102, 298
Jones, William E., 103, 302
Jordan, Thomas, 103, 302

- K -
Keitt, Lawrence M., 283
Kelly, John H., 103, 302
Kemper, James L., 29, 103, 298

Kennedy, John D., 29, 104, 302
Kershaw, Joseph B., 30, 104, 299
Keyes, Wade R., 46, 295
King, William H., 302
Kirkland, William W., 104, 302
Kitchen, Thomas, 290
Knox, Robert T., 277
Kurtz, Peter L., 255

- L -
Landvoigt, Ed, 227
Lane, James H., 104, 302
Lane, Walter P., 105, 302
Lanier, John S., 247
Lanier, Robert S., 13
Latrobe, Osmun, 247
Law, Evander M., 105, 299
Lawton, Alexander R., 26, 105, 302
Leach, Elijah S., 271
Leadbetter, Danville, 32, 105, 302
Lee, Edwin G., 106, 302
Lee, Fitzhugh, 27, 106, 298
Lee, George W. C., 24, 36, 106, 299
Lee, John G., 275
Lee, Robert E., 14, 24, 28, 30, 36, 106, 297
Lee, Stephen D., 24, 107, 297
Lee, William H. F., 24, 27, 107, 298
Leventhorpe, Collett, 107, 302
Lewis, Joseph H., 107, 302
Lewis, L. M., 302
Lewis, William G., 108, 302
Liddell, St. John R., 108, 302
Lilley, Robert D., 108, 302
Lincoln, Abraham, 11, 12, 15, 16, 21, 22, 28, 31, 33, 296
Little, Henry, 302
Little, Lewis H., 31, 32, 108
Logan, Thomas M., 30, 109, 302
Lomax, Lunsford L., 23, 29, 32, 109, 299
Long, Armistead L., 26, 109, 303
Longstreet, James, 26, 29, 31, 109, 297
Loring, William W., 110, 298
Love, Lucien, 269
Lovell, Mansfield, 32, 110, 298
Lowrey, Mark P., 24, 110, 303
Lowry, David, 228
Lowry, Robert, 27, 110, 303
Lumpkin, Tom, 254

Lynch, William F., 292
Lyon, Hylan B., 23, 111, 303

- M -
Mabry, Hinchie P., 303
Mackall, William W., 31, 111, 303
MacLay, Robert P., 303
MacRae, William, 111, 303
Madison, James, 25
Magruder, John B., 111, 298
Mahone, William, 112, 299
Major, James P., 23, 112, 303
Mallory, Stephen R., 44, 295
Maney, George E., 27, 31, 112, 303
Manigault, Arthur M., 112, 303
Mann, Theophilus, 261
Marmaduke, John S., 113, 298
Marshall, Humphrey, 113, 303
Marshall, Joseph K., 231
Martin, Albert B., 257
Martin, James G., 113, 303
Martin, John D., 303
Martin, William T., 113, 298
Marx, Karl, 33
Massie, Edmund L., 238
Maury, Dabney H., 25, 26, 114, 298
Maxey, Samuel B., 27, 114, 298
McCausland, John, 114, 303
McComb, William, 23, 32, 114, 303
McCown, John P., 115, 298
McCray, Thomas H., 303
McCreary, Thomas, 266
McCulloch, Benjamin, 115, 303
McCulloch, Henry E., 115, 303
McCulloch, James W., 271
McCutchan, James B., 267
McGowan, Samuel, 115, 303
McIlwaine, Frances S., 282
McIlwaine, Mary, 282
McIlwaine, Richard, 282
McIlwaine, Sarah, 282
McIntosh, James M., 116, 303
McKinley, William, 26, 27, 29, 31
McLane, Thomas S., 273
McLaws, Lafayette, 29, 116, 298
McMurray, James A., 303
McNair, Evander, 116, 303
McRae, Dandridge, 116, 303
McRorie, William F., 276
Memminger, Christopher G., 43, 295

Mercer, Hugh W., 117, 303
Miles, William R., 303
Miller, Francis T., 13
Miller, William, 117, 303
Millner, James W., 274
Moody, Young M., 117, 303
Moore, Henry A., 268
Moore, John C. (brigadier-general), 25, 117, 303
Moore, John C. (private), 229
Moore, Patrick T., 118, 303
Moore, S. P., 303
Moore, William S., 229
Morgan, John H., 118, 303
Morgan, John T., 27, 118, 303
Mosby, John S., 241
Mouton, Alfred, 303
Mouton, Jean J. A. A., 118
Munford, Thomas T., 303

- N -
Nail, Philip A., 279
Neblett, James H. M., 258
Nelson, Allison, 119, 303
Nelson, Thomas S., 277
Nicholls, Francis R. T., 29, 119, 303
Northrop, Lucius B., 119

- O -
O'Neal, Edward A., 29, 119, 303
Ott, William B., 272

- P -
Page, Richard L., 120, 303
Palmer, Joseph B., 120, 303
Parish, _____, 262
Parks, William P., 239
Parsons, Mosby M., 14, 120, 303
Paxton, Elisha F., 120, 303
Payne, Alexander D., 266
Payne, William H. F., 121, 303
Peatross, Robert O., 259
Peck, William R., 121, 303
Pegram, John, 121, 299
Pelham, John C., 260
Pemberton, John C., 25, 32, 121, 297
Pemberton, John S., 25
Pender, William D., 122, 298
Pendleton, Alexander S., 278
Pendleton, William N., 122, 303
Perrin, Abner M., 122, 303

Perrin, Achilles, 262
Perry, Edward A., 32, 122, 303
Perry, William F., 123, 303
Pettigrew, James J., 123, 303
Pettus, Edmund W., 29, 123, 303
Phifer, Charles W., 303
Pickett, George E., 35, 123, 298
Pike, Albert, 32, 124, 303
Pillow, Gideon J., 31, 124, 303
Polignac, Camille A. J. M., 124, 298
Polk, Leonidas, 124, 297
Polk, Lucius E., 27, 125, 303
Pollard, Stephen, 246
Posey, Carnot, 125, 303
Poteat, Charles L., 280
Powell, E. F., 160
Powell, John J. A., 276
Powell, William H., 259
Presgraves, William H., 257
Preston, John S., 125, 303
Preston, William, 14, 125, 299
Price, Adrian D., 281
Price, Felix L., 259
Price, Sterling, 126, 298
Pryor, Roger A., 126, 303
Purnell, George W., 242
Purnell, L., 255

- Q -
Quantrill, William C., 288
Quarles, William A., 126, 304

- R -
Rains, Gabriel J., 25, 126, 304
Rains, George W., 304
Rains, James E., 127, 304
Ramseur, Stephen D., 127, 299
Randal, Horace, 304
Randolph, George W., 43, 127, 295, 304
Ransom, Matt W., 26, 127, 299
Ransom, Robert, Jr., 128, 298
Rapier, John L., 290
Ray, J., 238
Ray, S. B., 286
Reagan, John H., 45, 295
Reece, John R. A., 281
Rees, Charles R., 19
Reid, John C., 304
Reid, Legh W., 230
Reynolds, Alexander W., 128, 304
Reynolds, Arthur E., 304

Reynolds, Daniel H., 128, 304
Rhodes, John J., 279
Richardson, Robert V., 128, 304
Rigby, John, 283
Ripley, Roswell S., 129, 304
Roane, John S., 129, 304
Roberts, William P., 129, 304
Robertson, Beverly H., 129, 304
Robertson, Felix H., 130, 304
Robertson, J. P. 272
Robertson, Jerome B., 130, 304
Robinson, Robert E., 286
Roddey, Philip D., 130, 304
Rodes, Robert E., 130, 298
Roosevelt, Theodore, 26, 29
Ross, Lawrence S., 25, 27, 32, 131, 304
Ross, Reuben R., 304
Rosser, Thomas L., 23, 31, 131, 299
Rowland, Joseph T., 258
Rucker, Edmund W., 14, 131, 304
Ruff, Charles H., 272
Ruggles, Daniel, 32, 131, 304
Russell, W. W., 304
Rust, Albert, 132, 304

- S -
Sanders, John C. C., 132, 304
Scales, Alfred M., 27, 132, 304
Scott, Thomas M., 23, 133, 304
Scurry, William R., 133, 304
Seabrook, Lochlainn, 2-3, 11-16, 21-35, 323, 325
Sears, Claudius W., 32, 133, 304
Seddon, James A., 44, 295
Sellman, John P., 243
Semmes, Paul J., 133, 304
Sharp, Jacob H., 134, 304
Shelby, Joseph O., 26, 134, 304
Shelley, Charles M., 26, 134, 304
Shields, Mrs. James, 161
Shindler, William P., 304
Shirley, Silas A., 268
Shoup, Francis A., 32, 134, 304
Sibley, Henry H., 25, 31, 135, 304
Simms, James P., 135, 304
Slack, William Y., 135, 304
Slaughter, James E., 25, 30, 135, 304
Smith, Archibald M., 239
Smith, B. F., 239
Smith, Edmund K., 136, 297

Smith, Gustavus W., 26, 44, 136, 295, 298
Smith, James A., 23, 136, 304
Smith, John L., 285
Smith, Martin L., 32, 136, 298
Smith, Preston, 137, 304
Smith, Thomas B., 137, 304
Smith, William, 28, 137, 298
Smith, William D., 137, 304
Sneed, John L. T., 304
Snodgrass, William, 254
Sorrel, Gilbert M., 26, 138, 304
Stafford, Leroy A., 138, 304
Starke, Peter B., 138, 304
Starke, William E., 138, 304
Steele, William, 32, 139, 304
Steen, A. D., 304
Stephens, Alexander H., 11, 30, 42, 295
Steuart, George H., 32, 139, 304
Stevens, Clement H., 32, 139, 304
Stevens, Walter H., 32, 139, 304
Stevenson, Carter L., 140, 298
Stewart, Alexander P., 24, 29, 140, 297
St. John, Isaac M., 132, 304
Stokes, Andrew J., 244
Stokes, Montfort S., 284
Stone, William, 275
Stovall, Marcellus A., 140, 304
Strahl, Otho F., 140, 304
Stuart, James E. B., 141, 298
Sutton, Robert B., 278
Swann, Christopher, 277
Sweet, Jonathan, 159

- T -
Taliaferro, William B., 14, 141, 299
Tappan, James C., 141, 304
Taylor, Richard, 25, 141, 297
Taylor, Sarah K., 25
Taylor, Thomas H., 29, 142, 304
Taylor, Walter H., 36
Taylor, Zachary, 25
Terrill, James B., 142, 305
Terry, William, 29, 142, 305
Terry, William R., 142, 305
Thatcher, David M., 254
Thomas, Allen, 29, 32, 143, 305
Thomas, Bryan M., 23, 29, 143, 305
Thomas, Edward L., 27, 31, 143, 305

Thompson, Augustus C., 159
Thompson, Daniel B., 283
Thompson, David, 263
Thompson, M. Jeff, 305
Thompson, Walter K., 228
Tilghman, Lloyd, 143, 305
Tinsley, Howard, 284
Todd, William B., 251
Toombs, Robert A., 28, 42, 144, 295, 305
Toon, Thomas F., 29, 144, 305
Tracy, Edward D., 144, 305
Trapier, James H., 144, 305
Trenholm, George A., 43, 295
Trimble, Isaac R., 145, 298
Tucker, William F., 145, 305
Turrentine, Daniel, 257
Twiggs, David E., 145, 298
Tyler, Robert C., 145, 305

- V -
Vance, Robert B., 27, 146, 305
Van Dorn, Earl, 31, 146, 298
Varnell, Benjamin W., 271
Vaughan, Alfred J., Jr., 23, 146, 305
Vaughan, Robert, 278
Vaughn, John C., 26, 31, 146, 305
Villepigue, John B., 147, 305

- W -
Wade, William B., 305
Walker, Henry H., 147, 305
Walker, James A., 27, 147, 305
Walker, John G., 27, 31, 147, 298
Walker, Joseph, 262
Walker, Leroy P., 43, 148, 295, 305
Walker, Lucius M., 23, 148, 305
Walker, R. Lindsay, 305
Walker, Reuben L., 23, 24, 148
Walker, William H. T., 148, 298
Walker, William S., 32, 149, 305
Wallace, William H., 27, 149
Walthall, Edward C., 27, 149, 299
Ward, W. P., 275
Ward, William W., 286
Waterhouse, Richard, Jr., 149, 305
Watie, Stand, 23, 150, 305
Watts, Thomas H., 46, 295
Waul, Thomas N., 150, 305
Wayne, Henry C., 25, 31, 150
Weems, Philip V. H., 285

Weisiger, David A., 150, 305
Wellmore, Henry Z., 286
Welsh, Warner G., 162
Wenner, C. C., 289
Wharton, Gabriel C., 27, 151, 305
Wharton, John A., 151, 298
Wheeler, Joseph, 26, 151, 297
White, Isaac, 256
White, James B., 287
Whitfield, John W., 28, 151, 305
Whitfield, Smith, 272
Whiting, William H. C., 152, 298
Whitten, Joshua, 262
Wickham, Williams C., 24, 31, 152, 305
Wigfall, Louis T., 28, 152, 305
Wilcox, Cadmus M., 26, 152, 298
Wilhelm, Samuel H., 253
Williams, John S., 23, 28, 153, 305
Williamson, George H., 260
Willich, August, 33
Willis, Edward, 305
Willis, William H., 284
Wilson, Claudius C., 23, 153, 305
Wilson, Robert M., 285
Winder, Charles S., 32, 153, 305
Winder, John H., 23, 30, 153, 305
Wingfield, Reggie T., 245
Winn, Achsah C., 283
Wise, Henry A., 14, 25, 28, 31, 154, 305
Wisenbaker, James A., 277
Wisenbaker, Sarah A. D. 277
Withers, Jones M., 28, 154, 298
Wofford, William T., 24, 154, 305
Wolff, Bernard L., 243
Wood, Sterling A. M., 24, 28, 154, 305
Wright, Ambrose R., 155, 299
Wright, Daniel G., 227
Wright, Gilbert J., 305
Wright, Marcus J., 26, 155, 305

- Y -
York, Zebulon, 32, 155, 305
Young, Bennett H., 16
Young, Pierce M. B., 155, 299
Young, William H., 156, 305

- Z -
Zollicoffer, Felix K., 156, 305

MEET THE AUTHOR

NEO-VICTORIAN SCHOLAR LOCHLAINN SEABROOK, a descendant of the families of Alexander Hamilton Stephens, John Singleton Mosby, Edmund Winchester Rucker, and William Giles Harding, is a 7th generation Kentuckian and the most prolific pro-South writer in the world today. Known by literary critics as the "new Shelby Foote" and by his fans as the "Voice of the Traditional South," he is a recipient of the prestigious Jefferson Davis Historical Gold Medal. As a lifelong writer he has authored and edited books ranging in topics from history, politics, science, and biography, to nature, religion, music, and the paranormal, books that his readers describe as "game changers," "transformative," and "life altering."

One of the world's most popular living historians, he is a 17th generation Southerner of Appalachian heritage who descends from dozens of patriotic Revolutionary War soldiers and Confederate soldiers from Kentucky, Tennessee, North Carolina, and Virginia. A proud member of the Sons of the Confederate Veterans, he is a true Renaissance Man. Besides being an accomplished and well respected author-historian and Bible authority, he is also a Kentucky Colonel, eagle scout, screenwriter, nature, wildlife, and landscape photographer, artist, graphic designer, songwriter (3,000 songs), film composer, multi-instrument musician, vocalist, session player, music producer, genealogist, former history museum docent, and a former ranch hand, zookeeper, and wrangler.

His over 70 adult and children's books contain some 60,000 well-researched pages that have earned him accolades from around the globe. His works, which have sold on every continent except Antarctica, have introduced hundreds of thousands to vital facts that have been left out of our mainstream books. He has been endorsed internationally by leading experts, museum curators, award-winning historians, bestselling authors, celebrities, filmmakers, noted scientists, well regarded educators, TV show hosts and producers, renowned military artists, esteemed heritage organizations, and distinguished academicians of all races, creeds, and colors. Colonel Seabrook holds the world record for writing the most books on Southern icon Nathan Bedford Forrest: 12.

Of northern and central European descent, he is the 6th great-grandson of the Earl of Oxford and a descendant of European royalty. His modern day cousins include: Johnny Cash, Elvis Presley, Lisa Marie Presley, Billy Ray and Miley Cyrus, Patty Loveless, Tim McGraw, Lee Ann Womack, Dolly Parton, Pat Boone, Naomi, Wynonna, and Ashley Judd, Ricky Skaggs, the Sunshine Sisters, Martha Carson, Chet Atkins, Patrick J. Buchanan, Cindy Crawford, Arthur Conan Doyle, Bertram Thomas Combs (Kentucky's 50th governor), Edith Bolling (second wife of President Woodrow Wilson), Andy Griffith, Riley Keough, George C. Scott, Robert Duvall, Reese Witherspoon, Lee Marvin, Rebecca Gayheart, and Tom Cruise.

A constitutionalist and avid outdoorsman and gun advocate, Colonel Seabrook is the author of the international blockbuster, *Everything You Were Taught About the Civil War is Wrong, Ask a Southerner!* He lives with his wife and family in beautiful historic Middle Tennessee, the heart of the Confederacy.

For more information on author Mr. Seabrook visit
LOCHLAINNSEABROOK.COM

"Teach your children that the proudest day in all your proud careers was that on which you enlisted as Southern soldiers."

Confederate Major-General Robert Frederick Hoke

FROM HIS FAREWELL MESSAGE TO HIS TROOPS
April 1865

LOCHLAINN SEABROOK ~ 325

If you enjoyed this book you will be interested in Colonel Seabrook's popular related titles:

- ABRAHAM LINCOLN WAS A LIBERAL, JEFFERSON DAVIS WAS A CONSERVATIVE
- EVERYTHING YOU WERE TAUGHT ABOUT THE CIVIL WAR IS WRONG, ASK A SOUTHERNER!
- ALL WE ASK IS TO BE LET ALONE: THE SOUTHERN SECESSION FACT BOOK
- EVERYTHING YOU WERE TAUGHT ABOUT AMERICAN SLAVERY IS WRONG, ASK A SOUTHERNER!
- CONFEDERATE FLAG FACTS: WHAT EVERY AMERICAN SHOULD KNOW ABOUT DIXIE'S SOUTHERN CROSS
- LINCOLN'S WAR: THE REAL CAUSE, THE REAL WINNER, THE REAL LOSER

Available from Sea Raven Press and wherever fine books are sold

  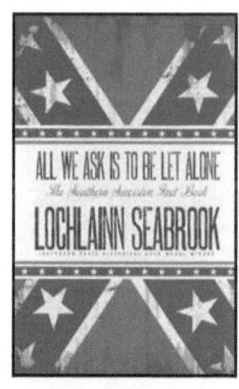

ALL OF OUR BOOK COVERS ARE AVAILABLE AS 11" X 17" COLOR POSTERS, SUITABLE FOR FRAMING

SeaRavenPress.com

www.ingramcontent.com/pod-product-compliance
Lightning Source LLC
Chambersburg PA
CBHW020324170426
43200CB00006B/263